Sequencing

Deciphering Your Company's DNA

Sequencing

Will your company
be innovative over
the long haul?

Michael Metzger

GCB

Game Changer Books

Sequencing: Deciphering Your Company's DNA

Copyright ©2010 by Michael Metzger

Published by:
Game Changer Books LLC
Waukesha, Wisconsin 53188

www.gamechangerbooks.com

Book design by Nat Belz

Printed in the United States of America

First Edition

ISBN 978-0-9826566-0-0

Library of Congress Control Number: 2010924340

To, my wife, Kathy,
my long-loved love
with whom
I have learned
"that with my own soul
I am out of tune…"

INNOVATE

From the Latin *innovatus*, "to renew or change"

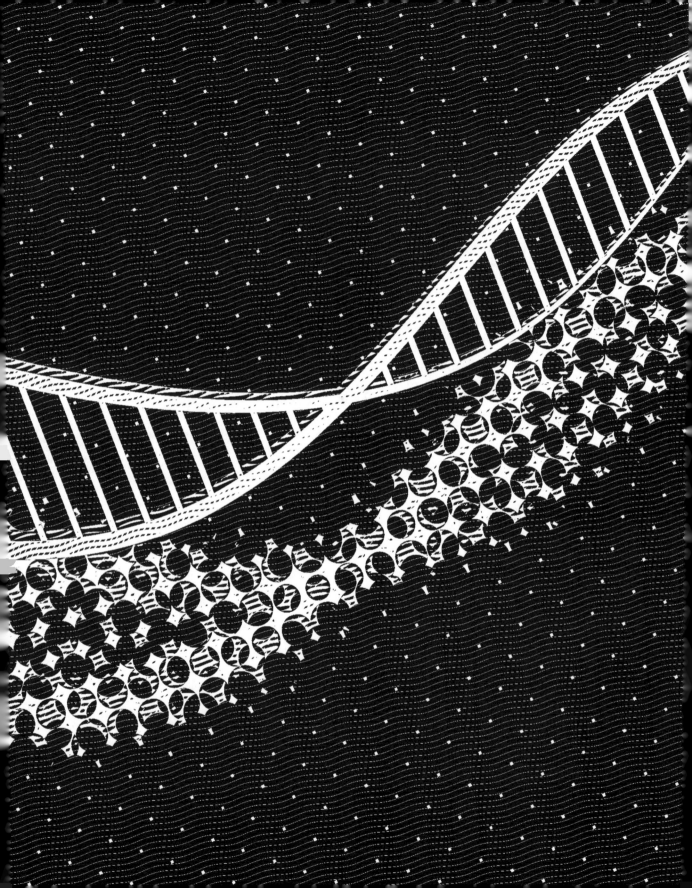

Foreword

David Kiersznowski

CEO, DEMDACO

The first time I had a long, sit down meeting with Mike Metzger was in the living room of my house in 2002. My bride Demi was there, along with several senior members of our company DEMDACO, and we were meeting with Mike for what I believed to be a meeting about business culture. Turns out I was incredibly nearsighted in my thinking.

A living room isn't necessarily a normal meeting spot for a business discussion. But I had heard Mike speak before, and had read some of his materials, and I knew that the location I chose for the meeting had to break the rules. Mike didn't grow up in the business world, and therefore hadn't fallen into many of the same traps that the rest of us had. Traps about what "business" was all about, and what a company culture should look like, and how to get there. I remember that Mike started talking to us about the formation of the United States of America, and the history of the industrial revolution, and I'm pretty sure he even brought in a bit of philosophy. I was absolutely bewildered after the first hour, and I was absolutely hooked. Because I knew Mike was trying to get us to go below the surface, to really examine our core beliefs about what our company should be about.

We had several common friends, and so Mike knew us well enough to know that we really did want to think seriously about the type of company we were creating. I knew of Mike's work enough to know that he wasn't going to start with a review of the most popular business trends. To some degree, I almost felt like that first meeting was almost a challenge to each other. Which side could go deeper in the discussion? Which could show the other that they cared more about what really mattered in a company, and less about what the latest fads were? After a several hour intense discussion on what matters most in a company and how leaders can best develop the culture and company they really want, I knew that the challenge was over. Mike had won the first round.

The last seven years have been nothing short of pure exhaustion and pure exhilaration for me. Our company, DEMDACO, has been a bit of a laboratory for Mike and The Clapham Institute.

Our entire senior leadership team has spent significant time wrestling with the challenge that Mike posed to us at the beginning: to pursue business as it ought to be. To be honest, the team was at the same time a bit cynical and a bit exhilarated by this idea of "ought." It's not a word we were using in our company, and it seemed almost too simple to be meaningful. And yet, at a soul level, it was a word that resonated with each and every one of us in a way that made us want to shout "bingo." I think it was the word all of us had hoped for, and perhaps was even the reason that some of our senior leaders joined DEMDACO. For the hope that we might pursue that which ought to be. But we needed *ought* to have traction, to be real.

That's probably one of the places that Mike challenged us the most. I think many of us were expecting that Mike would come in with a somewhat canned program. You know; give your associates these employee benefits, make sure you have employee picnics, and if you really want to hit the ball out of the park, perhaps even provide a free breakfast once a year with a guy who's good at flipping pancakes onto a paper plate. But what Mike was trying to get us to was not a canned program. Rather, he was trying to help us see reality more clearly, and for that I will be forever grateful. That was the home run for us; the concept that Mike calls "sequencing." It basically seeks to understand how and why organizations and their employees fundamentally interact, and this core understanding allows a company to get way below the surface, and pursue a company and a culture that truly is good. At its core. Because you understand the core, and how it works.

I'm not an infomercial guy; I tend to dismiss anything that can be bought quickly and provide meaningful change quickly. And so if your hope is that you might be able to simply read this book, and perhaps give it to some colleagues at work to read, and that your organization will magically change after that, I'd recommend you save your time. It won't work. There's too much unlearning and learning to be done by all of us who have grown up in organizations. However, if you're looking to begin the process of really thinking through how and why organizations tick, and how they can begin the process of becoming better places to work and live (or to borrow from the Greek philosophers, places that pursue the good, the true and the beautiful), then by all means read on.

This book will give you a glimpse into many, many years of real wrestling and significant research. And I hope reading this book does for you what these ideas have done for us. It's given us hope that perhaps organizations really can be good and really can be vehicles for good. We've developed a better understanding of the reality of our company, which has allowed us to pursue trying to become a better company each and every year. The singer Bono has been quoted with saying something that I absolutely love. During an interview he was asked about his amazing and tireless pursuit of social justice. His response was "Look, I'm just a singer. But in the end, I just want to tear a little corner off the darkness." I love that. To some degree I think that represents our hopes and dreams at DEMDACO. But we didn't really know how to get there. Our work with Mike over the past seven years has allowed us to clearly pursue these hopes and dreams, and has given us hope that perhaps we, too, can tear a little corner off the darkness.

Our first few years of DEMDACO (1997-2002) were, in many ways, typical first years for a company. We did some things right, and we did many things wrong. We had a group of, in my opinion, good people who wanted to do good things, but we had no framework to think about our organization. And we were struggling to keep up with a growing little company and the stresses that growth brought. We wanted to create a company that, at its core, was good, but we didn't really know what that looked like, or even what it meant. And then the meeting with Mike happened. And seven years have passed, and we're all both exhausted and exhilarated, and we think we're probably somewhere between the starting line and the finish line. And we're pretty sure that's where we'll always be, but hopefully moving slowly towards the finish line. Which is just fine with us, really, since we all love the ongoing process of writing the story of DEMDACO.

I remember Mike saying to me that he didn't really write *Sequencing*. Rather, *Sequencing* wrote him. I understand that now. Mike didn't bring a canned program to our company and our associates. He helped us see reality more clearly, and that understanding has given us a very real framework to pursue creating a company of good. We're not even close to being there. But with Mike's help and his ongoing challenges, our company has been energized to change in very real ways. My hope for you is the same. And my sincere thanks to Mike for working with our company to help us see reality clearly, so that we might attempt, in our own spheres of influence, to do the same; to "tear a little corner off the darkness."

Contents

THREE

SO WHAT?

Sequencing E=cc

FOUR

NOW WHAT?
Taking E=cc Seriously

EPILOGUE

Prologue

1

A BETTER DEFINITION OF REALITY

The instant I saw the picture my mouth fell open.

—*James Watson*, recalling the first time he saw Rosalind Franklin's X-ray diffraction pictures of DNA—a precursor to Watson and Crick's discovery of the code of DNA

They found it. Now came the hard part.

On February 28, 1953, Francis Crick walked into the Eagle pub in Cambridge, England, and made a stunning announcement. Crick and his associate, James Watson, had found the secret code. That morning, they had figured out the structure of deoxyribonucleic acid, or what is commonly known as DNA. For years, researchers had assumed there had to be some sort of biological code that governed all of life. The discovery of this structure meant that every human being carries common hereditary information.

But this wasn't the truly innovative part.

DNA is reality. It is what it is.

Deciphering the *sequence* of genes in DNA was the real innovation. The long-term benefits derive from the fact that DNA is based on a more accurate assessment of human biology. Before this discovery scientists had suspected that such a code existed. Once DNA was discovered, there was great enthusiasm for deciphering it. This process is called *sequencing*.

Sequencing became the work of the Human Genome Project. It set out to properly determine the order of the four nucleotide bases—adenine, guanine, cytosine, and

thymine—in a molecule of DNA. This work was completed in 2003, and has resulted in knowledge of sequences that has significantly accelerated biological research and made it possible to solve seemingly intractable problems. Recent research, for example, has pinpointed a gene that could dramatically improve predictions of who will develop Alzheimer's and at what age.

While sequencing has tremendous long-term benefits, most discoveries, over time, tend to overplay their hand. New frameworks become problematic when they claim to be determinative or predictive of *everything.* For example, DNA tells us *what* makes us tick. But does it explain *why* we do what we do? DNA might explain biological evolution, but does it adequately explain the behavioral evolution of most companies?

Consultant Jim Collins says most successful organizations go through five stages. The first is a hubris born of success. Achievement becomes a blinder in the undisciplined pursuit of more—the bigger is better myth. In this headlong pursuit, leaders begin to "explain away" problems and deny looming risks, imperiling the organization. As the company begins to decline, it enters a fourth stage—a reactionary search for salvation, the magic bullet or program that will get the company back on track. The fifth and final stage is what Collins describes as a capitulation to irrelevance or death. Game over.

But is this the only game in town? Is there another way to understand behavior? A great many people suspect so. "The public believes that science does not have, and cannot have, all the answers," writes Daniel Yankelovich, "and that other ways of knowing are also legitimate and important." This book is about knowing what is critical to the long-term success of truly innovative companies. It offers a better definition of reality. According to Max De Pree, the first responsibility of a leader is to define reality. *Sequencing* is a better way of doing this because it's drawn from our daily experiences. It starts with a code.

It's not a secret code.

This code is as plain as the nose on your face (which might be why so few notice it). If you're talking about economics, the code is there. History? Politics? How about yesterday's staff meeting? The code was there. Because this behavioral code is daily and demonstrable, it can connect us in ways that we have yet to imagine.

This code holds the same promise as the discovery of DNA. This behavioral code could reframe how companies do performance reviews, bonuses, and incentives. It could enhance how companies hire and help colleagues flourish. Sequencing could enrich firms, factories, and even our families since everyone—whatever creed, color, gender, or ethnicity—lives inside this code. Just as every human being carries common hereditary information, every company carries common behavioral information. Sequencing this code could bring people together as never before.

Bringing people together begins with getting everyone on the same page. The code can do this, even though most of your colleagues have never heard of it. But they *live* by it. That's why people are often surprised when they discover the code. The hard part is sequencing.

The reward for companies sequencing our "moral DNA" is that they gain an accurate assessment of human nature. This is critical to the long-term success of truly innovative companies.

The reality, however, is that most companies treat "corporate DNA" like cotton candy. It's wink-wink, nod-nod.

That's a problem.

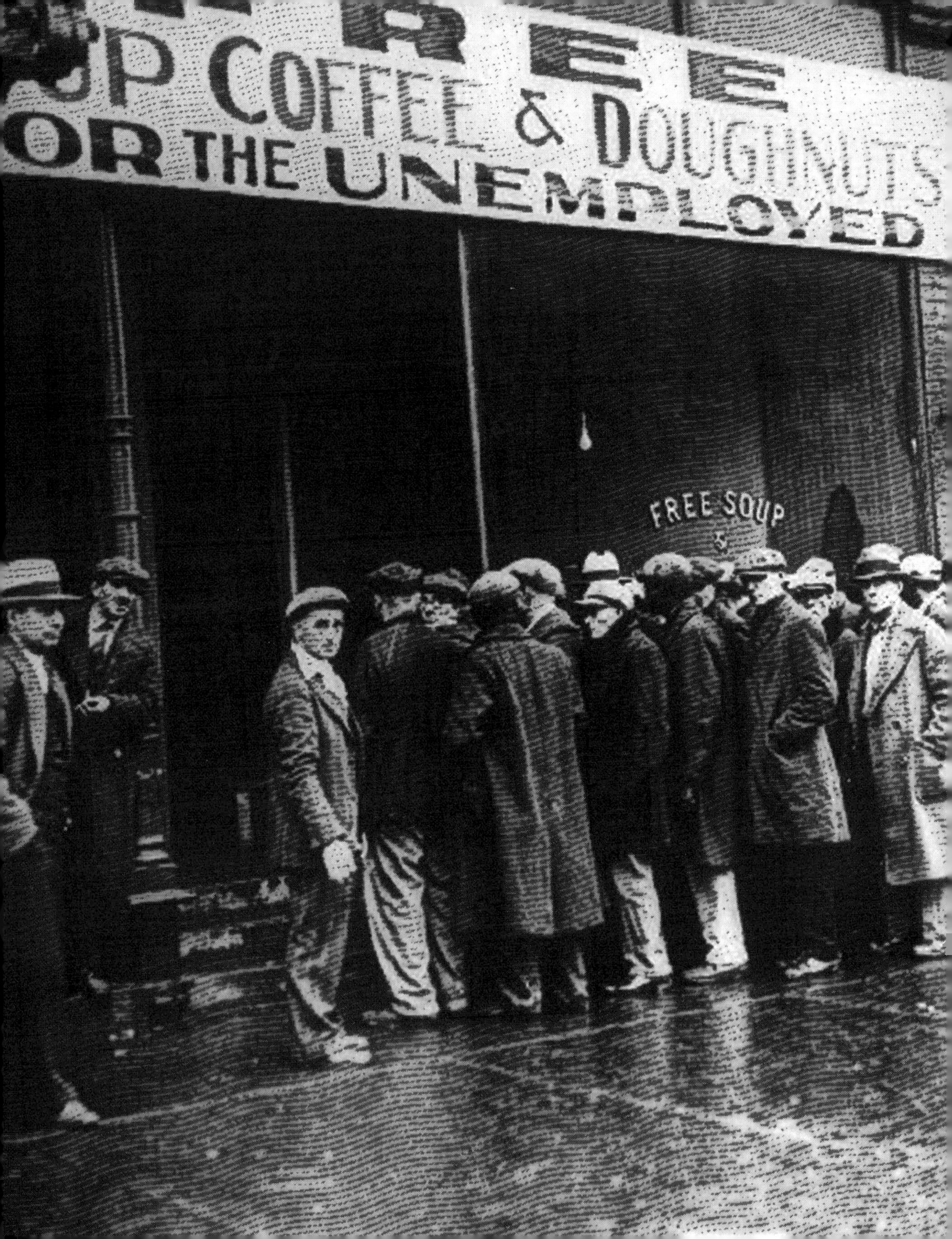
COFFEE & DOUGHNUTS
THE UNEMPLOYED
FREE SOUP

2

WINK-WINK, NOD-NOD

We are haunted, not by reality, but by those images
we put in place of reality.

—*Daniel Boorstin*

What business are you in?

Peter Drucker says the two diagnostic questions every organization must answer
are "What business are we in?" and "How's business?" *What business are you in?*
What is your organization's *ultimate purpose*? Your answer will suggest whether
your company takes its "moral DNA" seriously or treats it as absurd—as a wink and
a nod.

There is a difference between an organization's purpose and mission. *Mission*
is *what* an organization does. Patagonia's mission is selling outdoor apparel.
Purpose explains *why* an organization exists. Patagonia's purpose is environmental
activism. Mission statements describe *to-dos.* Purpose statements answer *what
for?* An organization needs both. They overlap, but over the last 40 years, purpose
statements like "restoring business" or "doing the right thing" have largely become
wink-wink, nod-nod. Shrewd people *know* the "real" business is merely making
money. Purpose statements? Whatever. The reality is that the economic crisis of
2008 is causing some to revisit Drucker's first question.

In his book *Managing in a Time of Great Change,* Drucker says that organizations
fail because, while doing many good things, "the assumptions on which the
organization has been built and is being run no longer fit reality." Remedies don't
work when they're not rooted in reality.

"It has rarely been clearer that the business of business is everyone's business,"

When is the last time you heard your company described as a "social institution?"

Yale University Professor Emeritus Alan Trachtenberg writes. The last time we faced a worldwide economic crisis—the 1930s—the answer to Drucker's first question was clearer: companies were "social institutions" as well as moneymaking enterprises. "This idea was not limited to mid-century intellectual opinion, but was central to the cultural scripts relating business corporations to the broader social order," researcher David Franz writes. As social institutions, companies had social obligations requiring moral language. Purpose statements reflected this. They were taken seriously.

When is the last time you heard your company described as a "social institution?"

The 1930s was the period when a new definition of reality emerged. The world was facing an economic crisis of unprecedented scale. Crises raise questions and often cause people to recalibrate their take on reality. It was during this period that economist Ronald Coase argued that corporations could dispense with the idea of being a social institution, reducing work to a "nexus of contracts between self-interested individuals." The corporation existed to turn a profit.

Slowly but surely, regardless of how the purpose statement read, everyone knew the real game was to maximize financial returns—to make as much money as possible. Corporate culture began to be treated as cotton candy. Maximizing financial return was elevated to the status of Holy Grail in 1970 when economist Milton Friedman wrote that the social responsibility of capitalism is to increase shareholder profit. Period. *The mission became the purpose*—making money. Lofty statements like "do the right thing" became platitudes or poster board material. *Finance* came to define the corporation. Financial statements found new importance as the bottom line for corporate existence. This became the *real* purpose of business.

This isn't a screed against spreadsheets. Max De Pree said it well: profits are like breathing. You don't live to breathe; but you have to breathe to live. However, once corporations became conduits for financial gain, talk of purpose wasn't taken seriously. "That's all fine, but corporate culture and ethics doesn't mean much if we aren't making money." That's true, as far as it goes. But how far does it go? Here's one way to find out.

Jack Welch said there's a defining moment when you can determine whether your organization takes its purpose statement seriously. In every company there are employees who don't embrace the purpose and aren't hitting the numbers. They're probably not in the right work. There are others who *do* embrace the values but aren't hitting the numbers. Counseling and mentoring might help. There is a third type who embraces the purpose and *is* hitting the numbers. That's a no-brainer. But here's the defining moment: What does your organization do when someone *doesn't* embrace the overarching purpose but *is* hitting the numbers?

It's the difference between a culture that is taken seriously or treated like cotton candy.

In too many instances, the fourth type of employee is seen as an archetype of success. This means talk of a "company DNA" and a moral compass doesn't translate into action when push comes to shove. Enron Corporation had a sixty-five-page ethics manual. How did that work out in crunch time? "To move into this area of business and moral and ethical behavior is to move into an area of double-talk and public-relations puffing," corporate planning consultant David Hussey writes. "It is an area of platitudes, or noble sounding statements which frequently have no bearing on the real way in which the business operates."

As a result, purpose statements or "values" are often treated as nice but not necessary. In 2005 the consulting firm Towers Perrin conducted a worldwide survey of tens of thousands of workers, asking if they really cared about the purpose statement of their company. The results indicate, "the vast majority of employees across all levels in an organization are less than fully engaged in their work." If purpose statements are to make good on their promises to connect companies and colleagues with a moral touchstone, they need to be seen as grounded in reality.

As we recover from this latest economic shockwave, even Greenspan now admits to a "flaw" in his thinking. Greenspan's mistake, by his own admission, was "presuming that the self-interest" of bank executives would best protect shareholders. If he had instead properly sequenced the code, he'd have seen ahead of time that many wouldn't.

Grounding corporate culture in reality means restoring companies and organizations to the way they ought to operate—innovation. If you're lost in the woods, you can't figure out which way to go if you don't know where you came from. What you assume to be advancement might be nothing more than activity. Without a fixed point to guide them, people walk in circles. So do companies.

Be careful, however. Before your organization begins to consider if it has the kind of culture that can innovate, make sure you're not whittling rotten wood.

3

WHITTLING ROTTEN WOOD?

Creativity requires the courage to let go of certainties.

—*Erich Fromm*

In 1983, General Motors tried to whittle rotten wood.

That was the year GM announced they were reinventing the car business. Saturn was a five billion dollar gamble in innovation. The fact that it took seven years for the first Saturn sedan to roll off the assembly line should have tipped off GM that trouble was looming ahead. Saturn was built around great ideas, including collaboration between labor and management and making the purchase of a car a dignified experience. Yet as Saturn went forward, GM's culture overwhelmed Saturn's innovations. GM was trying to whittle a new company from rotten wood.

As GM dealerships competed against Saturn,

investment money was steered away from the new enterprise. The models went stale. Labor relations went south. In the end, Saturn became just another GM brand, indistinguishable from the rest. Corporate cultures enable institutions to fail or flourish. Saturn is a story of the most critical challenge associated with innovation—too often it's whittling rotten wood.

Properly sequencing the moral DNA will restructure the core assumptions of an organization. Assumptions tend to become cherished beliefs in any institution. That's why most attempts to change a company's "corporate culture" go nowhere. In the end, Saturn was subsumed into GM's culture. Most organizations aren't up for innovation. They have a definition of reality that is not up for grabs. This definition then cements their assumptions, resulting in selective hearing.

Organizations tend to draw on research generally "in sync" with their presuppositions. But real innovation must always challenge bedrock principles. If an organization or business is not testing functional non-negotiables as rigorously as they should, they may tend too quickly to opt for resolutions that are not truly innovative. They're simply rearranging assumptions. That seems to be the case with General Motors and Saturn. The reality is that true innovation will disrupt the status quo. Human nature and history say it's an uphill battle.

In 1894, Italian Guglielmo Marconi invented a way to send messages through the air. It was an uphill battle after that. The Italian government turned down his offer of first rights because they saw no use for the technology. It didn't "fit" the way institutions imagined communication technologies. After all, Marconi's crude prototype could only send signals 100 yards—hardly a match for the increasingly popular landline telephone. Who would have known such a weak transmission method would pave the way for everything from television to mobile phones to texting to Twitter?

Marconi's wireless invention represents what Clayton Christensen calls "disruptive technologies." These are innovations such as the computer mouse, internal combustion engine, transistors, and Web browsers that not only create new industries but also disrupt the status quo. For example, the candle industry didn't invent the light bulb. In fact, electric lighting pretty much wiped out candle lighting. Makers of wall phones didn't invent the mobile phone. The reality of innovation is that it topples existing ideas and rewards innovation in the market economy—what Joseph Schumpeter called "the gales of creative destruction."

This is why success often becomes apparent only after the mess is cleaned up. For example, most people today hail mobile phones as an innovative improvement. But in the midst of innovation, they were wreaking havoc in the industry. It's why, in the maelstrom of real life messes, institutional leaders with established technologies tend to focus on making incremental improvements to their existing products and corporate cultures, avoiding the potential threat of truly innovative ideas and technologies. That was the case with GM and Saturn. Saturn was a disruptive technology. Changing GM's leadership culture was like whittling rotten wood.

To whittle a solid block of wood requires a solid block of leadership in an organization. All men (and women) are created equal, but not all are equal in creating culture. With a company's culture, there is a center and a periphery. The individuals *most critically involved* in the production of an organization's culture operate in the center where prestige is the highest—not on the periphery, where status is low. If corporate leaders are not serious about sequencing, the company is whittling rotten wood.

To be fair, the available wood carving tools might not be very good. Most of the business literature on "culture" is probably not worth the paper it's written on. This might be why, according to a recent survey conducted by *The New York Times*, the audience for the services of business consultants and the books they write is made up almost entirely of middle managers. Corporate leaders largely ignore books like this one.

But ignoring the moral dimension of business because the books are bad is like throwing out the baby with the bath water. "Bad books always lie," novelist Walker Percy wrote, "they lie most of all about the human condition." What we need are better books about human nature. Corporate America needs leaders who believe the unexamined life is not worth living—that sequencing our moral DNA is worth the effort. Socrates' maxim is probably the most quoted yet least followed statement from all antiquity. As a result, most workers find that their jobs are too small. We need leaders who pursue an examined life in an unexamining age and create companies with purpose.

Leaders are the ones to do this. Ed Keller and Jon Berry's findings indicate that 10 percent of the population determines what the other 90 percent eat, watch, and wear. They play the most critical role in *innovation*, which means "to renew or to change." Yet real innovation is rarely the work of only gifted individuals. Innovation happens largely through overlapping networks of ideas, images, items, institutions, and influential leaders. In other words, an institution is *not* the lengthened shadow of an individual. It is the lengthened shadow of networks. If we're going to increase the odds of long-term success of innovation, we have to change the cultures—plural—of many institutions. Leaders are in the best position to do this. If they are not on board, sequencing is simply whittling rotten wood.

Is your company up for innovation?

Is your leadership team ready to do the hard work of sequencing?

4

IS YOUR COMPANY UP FOR THIS?

> All human development, no matter what form it takes, must be outside the rules; otherwise we would never have anything new.
>
> —*Charles Kettering*

You can't be truly innovative if you're ignorant of human nature.

"Innovation" has been a buzzword in business literature for a long time. Yet the fact that in 1998 Enron was hailed as America's "most innovative company" should raise a few eyebrows. Why does long-term success for innovative companies often prove elusive? We could fill several pages listing "innovative" companies that have disappeared over the last few years alone, including Bennigan's, Worldcom, Lehman Brothers, Arthur Anderson, Bear Stearns, Global Crossing, and General Magic. What happened?

Most successful companies follow a bell curve—launching with an innovative mission, soaring into a movement, and then collapsing into a monument. In the 1950s, GM would have been considered an innovative company. The problem is innovation breeds insularity. Successful companies develop cultures where, after initial success at innovation, they act like the LAPD—"to protect and serve" the rule of law or the reigning definition of reality in the firm. Institutional leaders then dismiss whatever might be disruptive, embracing only those ideas that keep the machine humming.

This is one reason my father left GM in 1963. He believed the corporate culture was insular and out of touch with reality. Car buyers were drifting away from brand loyalty. They were demanding higher quality cars. When my father suggested these trends to GM leadership, they politely ignored him.

In 2000, Clayton Christensen reported on the failure rate in 350 companies that tried

"An institution is not the lengthened shadow of an individual. It is the lengthened overlapping network of ideas, images, items, and influential people."

to embrace and develop recognized disruptive innovations within their old culture. It was 100 percent. Success does not necessarily breed rotten leaders. But it often breeds rigidity. Leaders then unwittingly develop cultures that likewise become rigid. Disruption, however, is the lifeblood of innovation. Death brings forth new life. That's why companies have to pay attention to their culture. Cultures codify and concretize existing assumptions. They shape a company's "take" on reality. These assumptions reject disruption without thinking about it. It's why culture is the #1 inhibitor of innovation. Companies don't go bad because of a few bad apples. They go bad because of their culture.

There's a myth held by many CEOs that companies flop when they fail to root out a few bad apples scattered among the good. But what if that's not generally the case? What if the problem is usually in the orchard, in the soil or the soul of the corporation? What if sequencing a code, a behavioral DNA, could create a better orchard?

If this is reality, then it is critical that corporate leaders take seriously the entire enterprise of *making culture.* Cultures largely promote or prohibit innovation. They reflect a company's "take" on human nature. For example, David A. Kessler, a former commissioner of the Food and Drug Administration, says our culture encourages "conditioned hypereating." In *The Evolution of Obesity*, Michael L. Power and Jay Schulkin say the human body is now "mismatched" to human culture. But what if it's the other way around? What if the human culture is now "mismatched" to the human body?

In an age of obesity and global warming and economic hardship, this might be an opportune moment to recalibrate our take on reality. For example, how has your 401K performed recently? Two University of Chicago scholars, economist Richard Thaler and law professor Cass Sunstein, say most economic models ultimately fail because they're based on a faulty assessment of human nature. They're built on a defective definition of reality. You can't be truly innovative over the long haul if you're ignorant of human nature.

An *inaccurate* assessment of human nature might be why many "innovative" social programs are now coming under fire. In *NurtureShock*, Po Bronson and Ashley Merryman report on research indicating that convincing kids how smart they are is actually corrosive to their conduct and coursework. Telling kids to stay off drugs isn't working either. It has negligible short-term effects—nothing long-term, the authors report. Other researchers report that the whole tolerance and diversity movement passes right over the heads of young children and goes in one ear of young adults and out the other. In fact, university programs designed to improve racial sensitivity in students produce the opposite effect. "More diversity translates into more divisions between students," one researcher wrote. These programs are based on a deficient definition of reality. They're built on an inaccurate assessment of human nature; so the odds of long-term success are in doubt.

Perhaps most troubling is Kay Hymowitz's critique of *NurtureShock.* Hymowitz is a contributing editor at the Manhattan Institute and claims that the authors don't have the remotest idea how to translate such findings into constructive behavior or effective public programs. Sequencing can clear up some of the cluelessness. The findings reported in *NurtureShock* are the result of leaders relying on an inaccurate assessment of human nature. Albert Einstein said that you can't solve a problem using the same mind that created it. Your company can't enjoy long-term success at being truly innovative if it is operating inside old paradigms. Sequencing your company's behavioral DNA will provide a new paradigm—a better assessment of human nature.

Human nature tells us that people live primarily as enculturated beings, acclimated to their surrounding cultures more than they realize. When our friends from Florida come to visit, what once felt like warm autumn days are now said to feel like a wintry blast. They've become acclimated to Florida's balmy weather. Culture is like weather, which is why it is so influential. Since your colleagues will become enculturated to whatever culture your company develops, is your leadership committed to carving out the best culture possible?

We shape our cultures and then they shape us. The best cultures are based on an accurate assessment of human nature. In fact, as we sequence the code, you'll discover *the* critical characteristic of human nature that shapes a culture largely determines whether your company will enjoy long-term success at innovation.

Are you ready to begin sequencing?

The first step is answering a simple question. There are dozens of reasons why you work at your company: friendship, camaraderie, fulfilling the corporate mission or purpose statement, making good money, hoping to make *big* bucks, success, recognition, you name it. *But which one of these two ranks higher: fulfilling the corporate purpose statement* or *making good money?* Both are virtuous. Which one motivates you more? Write down your answer on a card and use it as a bookmark.

The answer you give goes a long way toward explaining whether you take corporate culture seriously or treat it like cotton candy. By the time you get to the close of this book, you'll see why.

Did you write down your answer? We'll review it at the end of this book.

Now, let's begin sequencing.

If you look closely at everyday life, you'll see a pattern explaining every nook and cranny of your company. Once you see the pattern, you'll see the key human quality that yields an accurate assessment of human nature. This characteristic is critical to the long-term success of truly innovative companies. Here we go.

ONE

SAY WHAT?

Seeing Reality

**The first responsibility
of a leader is
to define reality.**
—Max De Pree

5

THE LEAKAGE OF REALITY

You can't solve a problem with the same mind that created it.

—*Albert Einstein*

They had to blow up the spacecraft.

In 1999, NASA was forced to destroy the Mars Climate Orbiter as it entered the atmosphere of Mars. The problem—discovered later—was that the engineers were using two different sets of programming language to sequence the landing. Engineers at the Jet Propulsion Lab used metric measurements (newtons), while engineers at Lockheed Martin Astronautics in Denver—the prime contractor for the mission—had used English units (pounds) to measure the strength of thruster firings. As a result, the spacecraft began its orbit insertion into the Martian atmosphere at about 57 kilometers. It was intended to commence insertion at an altitude of 140 to 150 kilometers. At the low altitude of 57 kilometers, the orbiter would have disintegrated due to atmospheric friction. NASA was consequently forced to destroy the $125 million spacecraft.

The problem wasn't the data. The problem was the dialogue—the language engineers used to calibrate the landing sequence. They were using two different sets of programming language. The engineers ended up talking past one another.

Face it, most of the time we're no different. We regularly talk past one another. It's a major factor in all of our relationships—with our spouses, our children, our employees, our bosses, our neighbors, our political rivals, and our global competitors. We're good at dealing with data but lack a shared language that makes sense for everyone. The code can help solve this problem. It's a way of defining reality in a language that *everyone is already using.*

Sequencing is not just business; it's personal

This code is not, however, a contrived cryptogram. It's knowledge of reality. That's critical since present-day reality in companies often sounds like a cacophony of confused categorizations. We need a better definition of reality. If you need an example, look no further than today's younger people. According to Mark Bauerlein, a professor of English at Emory University, the younger the age, the worse the confusion.

Bright, intelligent, hardworking college students increasingly demonstrate an inability to sort through the onslaught of information that is so easily accessed by Web-based learning. College students find it hard to derive any coherence or meaning. Bauerlein says only 16 percent of today's students read the text on a Web page line by line, word for word, and can pull together a coherent summary of what the author intended to say. The other 84 percent can only pick out individual words and sentences, "processing them out of sequence." That's sobering, since the code is a sequence for reality. It's essential that people demonstrate some ability to deal with abstract thought if they are to understand the code. Students need a sequence for reality. So do companies and Congress, where a shared sense of reality seems to be escaping us.

When No Child Left Behind was enacted, for example, it decreed that by 2014 *all* American students would be proficient in math and reading. This piece of legislation was part and parcel of what the late senator Daniel Patrick Moynihan called "the leakage of reality from American life." The code can solve this problem. It's reality. It can plug the leak and recalibrate reality in such a way that students and senators and CEOs can make sense out of daily stuff.

What do we mean by "daily stuff"?

It's a dumbed-down way to describe the reality of a company or country's ups and

downs. For example, in the United States, we're living in an age of unprecedented problems pressing against audacious hopes. We need a shared language to solve our problems.

Almost two million people crammed onto the Washington, D.C. Mall to watch the swearing in of the nation's first African American president. Hundreds of millions around the world watched this historic event, raising hopes for a new age of American leadership. President Barack Obama has written eloquently on "the audacity of hope" and has called on Americans to accept personal responsibility for fixing our national and worldwide problems. This call has already elevated America's standing in the world. People are tired of the old tirades and political polarity. They're hoping this administration will find better ways of solving our deepest problems.

The problem is that a great many in Washington are locked into the old political divisiveness. Hope curdles into hype when real problems are not being solved. We can't solve these problems using the same equations that created them. No matter how many ways you rearrange the numbers, one plus two plus three will always equal six. You have to add something new to the old equation, or subtract something from it, or throw it out altogether to get a different result. Insanity is doing the same thing over and over and expecting a different result. Innovative solutions require a new sequence.

A new solution would require a more accurate assessment of human nature and reality.

One way to understand this new equation is to observe the consequences of the cultures it creates. Look at the last decade—Enron, WorldCom, Bear Stearns, and so on. The code is our behavioral reality, just as DNA is biological reality. Can't get over it, can't get around it. Sequence it properly or suffer the consequences.

Your company has a moral DNA. You can decipher a better culture or you can keep running on whatever default culture is currently in place. Better institutions make better individuals because they are better aligned with reality. This means that what you are about to learn—sequencing—works in financial firms, factories, fraternities, and even families. Reality is reality. There are not different realities; there is only your ability to decipher the current culture of your company. When you sequence the code, a company's DNA, you'll have an accurate assessment of human nature that is critical to the long-term success of truly innovative companies.

It starts by discovering the code. It's right there in front of you. All you need to do is simply sequence your daily experiences. For example, imagine something happening to your dream car. Or remember how you reacted to the events of 9/11.

6

BMWs, 9/11, AND A FRIEND NAMED BILL

The real voyage of discovery lies not in finding new lands, but in seeing with new eyes.

—*Marcel Proust*

Do we need a new pair of glasses?

G. Clotaire Rapaille is a French-born consultant with a doctorate in medical anthropology. He makes a great deal of money traveling the globe for corporate clients (Chrysler, Procter & Gamble, Boeing, and DuPont, to name a few), explaining what makes a country and its people tick. Armed with psychoanalytical theory, Rapaille believes there is a "code" for each culture. "The code is like an access code . . . once you get the code, you understand everything. It's like getting new glasses."

Rapaille, however, is not without his detractors. Some view it as amateurish psychology. Yet his corporate portfolio is as extravagant as his black velvet suits and Rolls-Royces, and he's not shy about boasting that "50 of the Fortune 100 companies" are his clients. Companies pay Rapaille between $125,000 and $225,000 to crack cultures, product categories, or brands across cultures. He gets $30,000 per forty-five-minute speech. At these rates, he must be on to something.

He is.

Rapaille is right about one thing—there is a code. It frames our home lives and the headlines around the world. The code goes beyond culture. It's global. It can be discovered in dramatic sagas or in daily stuff.

The code, in other words, is based in common sense.

The easiest way to explain the code is by experiencing it. Imagine, for example, that you

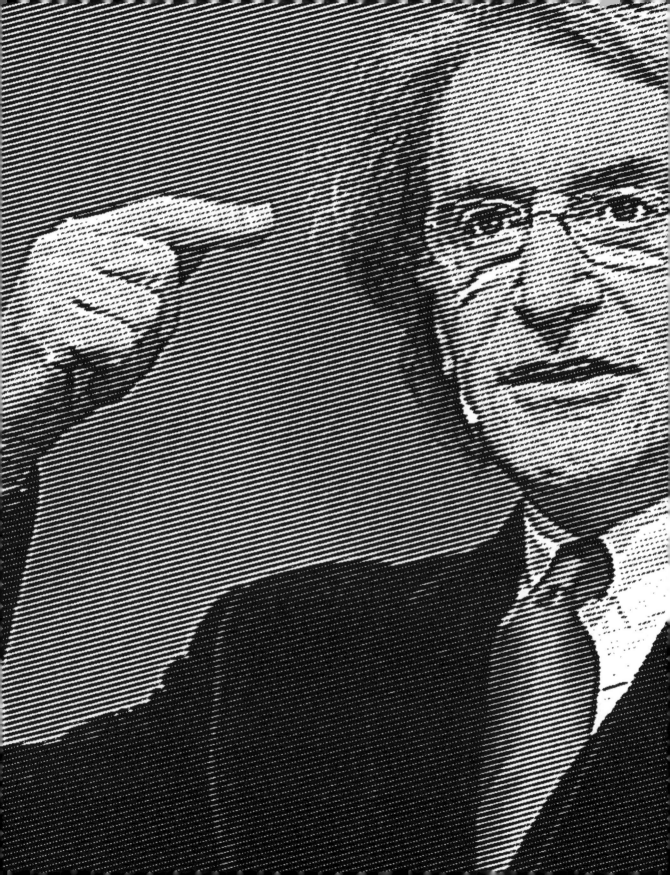

owned a Mystic Blue Metallic Clearcoat 5 Series BMW. Convertible, leather trim, all the bells and whistles. Sweet.

Now imagine you drive your new BMW to work, park it diagonally—just like Corvette owners—so that no one will dent your doors. At the end of the day, you leave work only to discover someone has run his keys across your car. How would you react? What would you think? What would you do? What would you scream—that is, if your kids and spouse were not within earshot?

Everything you'd feel, think, say, and do in this situation is *the code.*

It's right there in front of you. See it?

You can see the code in our corporate institutions. Imagine a company team that is managing what is currently the largest project under development. This company has enjoyed a profitable run over the last decade. Growth has ranged between 15 and 25 percent annually. Anticipating increasing revenues into the foreseeable future, they've recently completed several capital improvements, including building a new headquarters, expanding warehouse facilities, and enlarging the sales and marketing team. While a bit exposed, the company anticipates rolling out several new product lines that are expected to produce. You're part of the team the company is counting on. But things are not going well.

The product-development people have been tardy, their work is substandard, and they are missing deadlines. These knuckleheads show up late, sipping their sissy Starbucks lattes and fiddling with their iPhones. If things don't improve, layoffs are inevitable—including yours!

What would you *feel, think, say* to them, and perhaps *do* to them? If you record your feelings, thoughts, and actions, you'd see the code right there in front of you. As my dad loved to say, "I kid you not." In fact, the code can be found in how Johnson & Johnson responded to the Tylenol crisis in 1982.

In 1982, Tylenol® was the most successful over-the-counter product in the United States with over one hundred million users. But in the fall of that year, several Tylenol Extra-Strength capsules were laced with cyanide in resealed packages and deposited on the

shelves of at least a half-dozen or so pharmacies and food stores in the Chicago area. The poisoned capsules were purchased and seven unsuspecting people died.

The good news is that Johnson & Johnson had a company culture with concrete plans in the eventuality of such a crisis as this. Their actions followed the code. There *is* a code. But don't believe me—consider your reactions to the shocking events of 9/11.

Almost everyone can recall exactly where he or she was and what they were doing on the morning of September 11, 2001. I was driving to a conference on Maryland's Eastern Shore. When I arrived at the conference center, one of the staff mentioned that a plane had hit the World Trade Center. I immediately imagined something similar to what happened in 1945, when the pilot of a B-25 bomber became disoriented while flying over Manhattan. The medium-size plane smashed into the 78th and 79th floors of the Empire State Building, ripping a hole 18 feet wide and twenty feet high, killing 14 people (it was a fog-shrouded Saturday morning—there were few people at work or on the streets shopping). I imagined something along the same lines—a small, privately owned plane accidentally hitting the World Trade Center.

You can imagine my shock when I walked into the conference and saw everyone huddled around the television.

How did you feel? What did you think, say, or do when you witnessed the second jet crashing into the World Trade Center? If you do the mental math—computing every emotion, thought, and action—you'd have the code.

It's the same code that made sense of my friend Bill's life.

Bill was a successful businessman. He was making loads of money. And he was trying to ship a large portion of his good fortune offshore. And he was hooking up with a woman who was now doing a spot-on imitation of Glenn Close in *Fatal Attraction*. Yikes. Brazen and bound—not a great combination. We began to catch lunch every week. I listened, and he divulged. After several weeks, Bill asked my opinion: *What did I think of all this?* I replied, "Do you see the code? You're wrestling with it."

Did you see the code?

The code is in every one of the four stories you just read.

"The real voyage of discovery lies not in finding new lands, but in seeing with new eyes," Marcel Proust wrote. The code is something everyone can see. It's the DNA of every organization and individual. When you sequence it, you see the key characteristic that yields a better definition of reality. Ready to see the code?

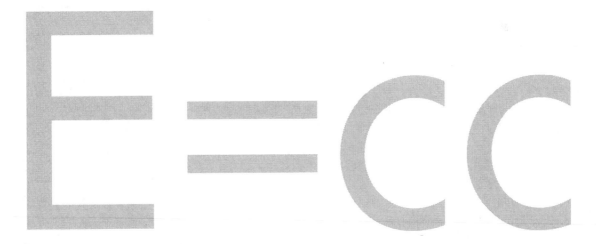

7

THE CODE

Addition is the exercise of fools. Subtraction is the exercise of genius.

—*Tom Peters*

Apparently some people can see the big picture better than others.

In 2006, Washington University scientists Desiree White and Richard Abrams reported on an uncanny similarity between the immortal Babe Ruth and St. Louis Cardinals slugger Albert Pujols. In 1921, when Ruth was twenty-six and at the top of his game, he was put through a series of tests ranging from finger tapping to visual responses to bat speed. When Pujols was twenty-six, he too was a top hitter in the game. Tests similar to Ruth's were administered to Pujols in 2006. Not only are Ruth and Pujols the only two baseball players to have ever aced the tests but they share a common trait that accounts for why they flourished as athletes.

The tests given to Pujols included putting a piece of paper in front of him with capital letters strewn about the page. White told Pujols to locate and cross out all of the A's. While most people scan a page left to right, Pujols instinctively divided the page into sectors and searched one briefly for the letters before moving on to the next sector. The result, according to White, is that Pujols—just like Babe Ruth eighty-five years earlier—can scan the whole field of play and see the big picture at an instant without missing any action. This accounts for Ruth and Pujols' extraordinary successes. It also explains why, according to Carl Jung, particular people flourish as human beings.

In 1928, Carl Gustav Jung, the founder of analytical psychology, suggested there are "big pictures" for life embedded in our mind—he called them *archetypes.* Some see these archetypes dimly, others with greater clarity. But the better we understand them and their sequence, the more we enjoy purpose in life. Jung believed these archetypes provide a "universal collective unconscious" that plays an active role in our development, whether we know it or not. They shape the way we see our entire lives.

The code is the big picture in the stories of the BMW, the product-development team's lagging performance, the 9/11 attacks, and Bill's personal conundrums. Start with your scarred BMW.

You'd first be *shocked* or *stunned*. Put that in your first mental column. Next you'd be *angry* or *pissed off*. Put that in the second cranial column. Of course, you'd want the person caught. Put that in the third column. Last, you'd *hope* that your BMW would be restored. Put that in the fourth column. There's the code.

Parse how anyone reacts to the development team's lagging performance. Everyone everywhere reports feelings of anger or frustration. Everyone will want to give them a piece of their mind. And they'd talk about what they'd do to fix the problem. Last, caring people hope for the best.

In corporate settings, I record these responses on a white board. They always organize themselves into four categories. Feeling *shocked, frustrated,* or *resentful* falls naturally into the first column—how things *ought* to be. *Anger* goes into the second column—the way life *is. Fixing a problem* falls into the third cranial column characterizing what people *can* do. *Hope* fits in the fourth column—how we hope things *will* turn out.

Obviously these four columns overlap and intersect, like four chapters in a book. But all four, combined, encapsulate the code.

At first, some don't see it. So I write a different word over each of the four columns. Beginning at the far left and over the first column of *frustration* and *shock,* I write: "OUGHT." Then I move one category to the right. Over *angry* and *pissed*, I write: "IS." Over the third column, with words like *fix it,* I write: "CAN." To the far right, over the fourth column, I write: "WILL." There's the code.

It's *ought-is-can-will.*

Whether we're talking about building cities or Citroëns, raising families or raising Cain, bickering with kids or colleagues, directing a symphony or sales meeting, or repairing a hole in the roof or hole in a heart, everyone's life reads like a book with four chapters—*ought-is-can-will.*

This code explains why Johnson & Johnson halted Tylenol production and advertising, issued a nationwide recall of Tylenol products (removing an estimated 31 million bottles from circulation with a retail value of over $100 million) and offered to exchange all Tylenol capsules already purchased by the public with solid tablets. That's what good companies ought to do. They imagined "what if," codified actionable steps, and inculcated them throughout the company.

This is the same code that explained every struggle in my friend Bill's life.

Bill imagined that he ought to be wealthy and randy. "It's not working out," he confessed. "What can I do?" I told Bill that the choices he made went a long way toward determining the kind of man he *would* become. Ought-is-can-will. Bill got it.

Over the course of our lunches, Bill began to sequence how his work, friendships, sex life, money, and affluence ought to be arranged. He considered why it is often the case that they're screwed up. "Bill, do you see how you can change your life?" I asked. He was beginning to. He had a new equation to sequence. It began to change how his life might turn out. Ought-is-can-will.

"He who has a *why* to live can bear with almost any *how,*" Friedrich Nietzsche wrote. Seeing the code sounds the starter's gun for understanding *why* we do *what* we do. Sequencing it will yield the key characteristic of human nature that is critical to the long-term success of truly innovative companies.

But I can already tell you whether you'll eventually take sequencing seriously. Ask yourself this: When you first saw the code, did you think, *Huh?* If you did, was it followed by an *Aha!* moment? If so, that's promising. Your responses indicate that the right hemisphere of your brain lit up. You experienced the "doggie head tilt." This kind of experience creates people who take sequencing seriously.

8

DOGGIE HEAD TILT

The idea came to me, without anything in my former thoughts seeming to have paved the way for it.

—Henri Poincaré

Henri Poincaré's flash of insight arrived as he boarded a city bus.

It worked in a similar fashion for Albert Einstein. His epiphany came as he imagined a boy riding alongside a light beam. In both instances, Poincaré's and Einstein's, insight started after a surprise, not a search. On occasion, people don't see the code because they're *trying* to see it. Board a bus instead, or ride a light beam. The point is, get the doggie head tilt before you start sequencing.

Poincaré was the nineteenth-century mathematician whose insights advanced non-Euclidean geometry. But his work didn't go forward until he *stopped* thinking about mathematics and simply boarded a bus. "At the moment when I put my foot on the step," Poincaré wrote, "the idea came to me, without anything in my former thoughts seeming to have paved the way for it . . . upon taking my seat in the omnibus, but I felt a perfect certainty." Boarding a bus led to Poincaré's *Aha*! epiphany.

People rarely learn new things by hunkering down over data. Einstein unlocked the mysteries of electromagnetic field equations discovered by James Clerk Maxwell years earlier. But at the moment of discovery Einstein wasn't delving into Maxwell's theory as much as daydreaming about light beams. Taking a break from investigative work led to Einstein's insight. Arresting or stopping the left-brain analytical process opens the pathways for what I call the "doggie head tilt."

"Doggie head tilt" is my singular talent—I can simultaneously hum and whistle. When I make this sound, dogs stop dead in their tracks and tilt their heads. *Arf? Huh?* It's like a stun gun to the left hemisphere of the brain. But why in heaven's name would you want to do this—stop the "left brain" in its tracks?

The left hemisphere of a human brain excels at information, according to Mark Jung-Beeman, a cognitive neuroscientist at Northwestern University. The right hemisphere deals with insight. It helps you see the forest for the trees. When Poincaré was mentally stuck and hopped a bus—a mindless activity for him—the left hemisphere of his brain relaxed and his right half was revving. *Huh?* Bang! Insight! *Aha!* When Einstein dreamed about light beams, blood had shifted to the right hemisphere. *Huh?* Bang! Insight! *Aha!* When I get behind the wheel of a car—an essentially mindless activity for me—blood leaves the left hemisphere and floods the right. Insights start to ignite. Of course, if driving becomes a *completely* mindless activity, Bang!

This approach contradicts the classic model of *focusing on facts,* says John Kounios, a cognitive neuroscientist at Drexel University. Focus is about blocking stuff *out.* It only activates the left hemisphere. You can't solve a problem in the left-brain frame that created it. "There's a good reason Google puts Ping-Pong tables in their headquarters," Kounios adds.

Fun and games loosen the left's lock on your noggin'. It's like hitting a baseball. Gripping the bat too tightly makes your arm muscles tighten, crimping your wrists and slowing your bat speed when striking the ball. Focusing on facts gives the left hemisphere of your brain too tight a grip and crimps the right, slowing the speed of insight. Insight and innovation generally come from the unexpected experience. Film and storytelling in general thrive on an element of the unexpected. They're great ways to activate the right hemisphere of the brain.

In fact, film and stories are why Arab youth feel deep hostility toward Americans.

During her tenure as ambassador to Morocco, Margaret Tutwiler discovered that the average day for a Moroccan man went like this: work hard all day, come home in the evening, unplug the car battery, haul it into the house and connect it to the TV so that the family can spend a mindless evening

together—just like Americans do. The left hemisphere shut down and the right is activated. Uh-oh.

At that time, *Baywatch* was the most widely watched TV show in Morocco. Many Moroccans assumed *Baywatch* was a Discovery Channel–type show documenting life in America. They initially reacted: *Huh?* Then, Bang! Insight! *Aha!* Arab youth assumed they'd gained new insight into American life. As a result, they felt deep hostility toward the United States.

This was the finding of a 2003 report on Arab youth attitudes, according to researchers Margaret and Melvin DeFleur. Arab youth imagine Americans as violent, prone to criminal activity, materialistic, and sexually immoral. "You can't turn on your television set on any night or go to a movie without seeing unmarried people cavorting in bed," they wrote, "or you can see folks with no clothes on, and so on, particularly women." Their study revealed that American movies and television programs are the primary sources shaping Arab hostility toward the United States—not foreign policy. When the Screenwriters Guild reviewed the DeFleurs' report, they suggested the title be changed to "We Hate You, But Please Send Us Baywatch!"

The *Huh?* preceding the *Aha!* is what educators call "incidental learning." For example, most kids go to movies or rent videos to be entertained. The directors and producers who make the films and videos may not intend to teach moral lessons anymore than Arab youths intend to come out imagining Americans as evil people after watching *Baywatch.* Arab youth aren't stupid. But film appeals more to right-brain learning. A good story always has an element of surprise. When Arab youth watched *Baywatch,* they assumed they were gaining new insights—right or wrong—into American life.

Insight is what excites CEOs and educators to take the code seriously and sequence it. Information doesn't. When you first saw the code, did you experience the "doggie head tilt"? If you did you'll likely sequence the code for your company.

If, however, you didn't say *Huh?*, try *listening* for the code instead. Maybe that will do the trick.

9

DO YOU HEAR WHAT I HEAR?

I got the music in me.

—*The Kiki Dee Band*

Your ears might be a better way to see your company's code.

If you play a note on a piano—say, a middle C—what you hear fills the whole of your *heard space*, writes Jeremy Begbie, a gifted musician and a professor at Duke University. Then, if you play a *second* note along with the middle C, that second note also fills the whole of your heard space, the same space as the C. Yet you hear the notes as distinct from each other. This phenomenon is called *aural perception*. The ear tells us that things *can* be in the same place at the same time—an important distinction when it comes to the code. Some imagine it as four chapters in a book. That's one way to look at it. But you might be someone who needs to *hear* the code.

In Western tonal music, there is a structure that goes like this: equilibrium-tension-resolution. It's in hundreds of thousands of songs and consists of a melody in a home key, followed by a move away, and then a return to the melody in the home key. If you don't believe it, sing "The Star-Spangled Banner" and try stopping abruptly after "through the perilous night." Doesn't work, does it?

This structure is derivative of the code. Any tune, even the silly 1976 hit "Play That Funky Music," has a structure of equilibrium-tension-resolution or orientation-disorientation-reorientation. "Funky" is part of the Western tonal music that emerged in the seventeenth century in Europe and has been predominant in European culture and in societies shaped by modern Europe. "It is the tradition of Beethoven and Bach, Rachmaninoff and the Grateful Dead, Zoltán Kodály and Girls Aloud," Begbie writes.

Music starts with an assumption of what life ought to be like (home) followed by a disjunction or tension (the way it is) and then coming home (what can happen) or being home again (what will happen). This musical homecoming is not a simple "back to the beginning," Begbie writes, but the culmination of a journey. *Ought-is-can-will.* From Bach to Brahms, R.E.M. to Eminem, the code is heard every day in almost every tune.

"Music is sound organized by rhythm (the tempo in time), melody (the linear arrangement of tones), harmony (the simultaneous sounding of different tones), texture (the affect of the composite arrangement of tempo and tones), and structure (the design of the piece as a whole)," writes cultural analyst John Seel. "Thus, music is sound arranged in time for the purpose of expressing meaning and beauty that connects with the human imagination and points to a transcendent origin. Because music is physical in nature, one's view of music is necessarily a reflection of one's view of reality—the true, good, and beautiful." Aural reality, words and music, is derivative of a deeper reality.

We can hear the code in music. Yet the reality is that it is mostly right-brain individuals and institutions that hear the code and sequence it. They might be Corporate America's best hope for the future.

In his bestseller *A Whole New Mind,* Daniel Pink says, "the future belongs to a different kind of person." He says it will be shaped by "designers, inventors, teachers, storytellers—creative and empathetic right-brain thinkers whose abilities mark the fault line between who gets ahead and who doesn't." Pink believes right-brain people are critical because they exhibit "the capacity to detect patterns and opportunities, to create artistic and emotional beauty, to craft a satisfying narrative . . ." This is a book for right-brain, creative individuals and institutions that want to craft a new and satisfying narrative.

Sequencing is for those companies and organizations that hear *ought-is-can-will* in the music of life. They see the code as grounded in social behavior and reality. This is what psychologist Robert Cialdini calls "social proof." It's perhaps the most powerful reason why some people and organizations do the hard work of sequencing.

Cialdini is a social psychologist and a professor at Arizona State University who has studied how social proof motivates people to take care of the environment. A few years ago, he conducted a study in a handful of Phoenix hotels comparing the effects of hotel-bathroom placards that ask guests to reuse towels. Cialdini tested four slightly different messages. The first was the standard "do it for the environment." The results were so-so. The second placard was an appeal to "cooperate with the hotel." It yielded better results. The third hotel placard asked guests to "be our partner in this cause" (stating that the majority of guests in the hotel reused towels at least once during their stay). "Partnering" proved more effective than "cooperation," and "cooperation" was more effective than "do it for the environment." The fourth message, however, was even more effective.

The fourth placard said that the majority of guests "in this room" had reused their towels. Cialdini says that when people were made aware of the social norm, they tended to adhere to it. He terms this effect "social proof." Individuals and institutions are most likely to respond to appeals grounded in social behavior and reality.

Ought-is-can-will is reinforced by social behavior but is grounded in reality. Social proof makes it more plausible. It's the music playing in our heads. Discovering it is a *Huh?* for some people. If they then experience an *Aha!*, they are more likely to sequence the code. Why? Insight comes from unpredictability. High predictability, low impact. Low predictability, high impact.

If the code grabs you, you'll likely sequence it. Deciphering your company's DNA will immediately yield the key characteristic that is critical to long-term success. It has to do with sequencing *ought plus is*. If you do the math, you find out: *Who cares about this code?*

Ought-Is-Can-Will

TWO

WHO CARES?

Sequencing Reality

Human beings, all over the earth, have this curious idea that they ought to behave in a certain way, and can't really get rid of it.

—C. S. Lewis

10

THE GREAT DEMARCATION

> The search is what anyone would undertake if he were not sunk in the everydayness of his own life.
>
> —*Walker Percy*

Curtis understands more than he knows.

Curtis deals with difficult situations every day. He's a plant supervisor who was participating in a sequencing session I was leading. "Listen, I deal with crap all day. That's the way it is. *That's* reality—it is what it is. I do what I can, and have to wait to see what will fall out. Your company code is neither here nor there—life is what it is."

I know the feeling. Many times we're so mired in the everydayness of our own lives that the code seems like nothing more than vowels and consonants. I asked Curtis if he enjoyed dealing with crap all day: "Is that the way it *ought* to be?" He said, "No, work ought to not feel crappy." "Well, Curtis, you just added *ought* to your definition of reality."

Sequencing doesn't start with "whatever is, is." *Ought* is the note that starts the sequence. *Is* acknowledges our ups and downs. *Can* is human action—what we do about the ups and downs. *Will* captures our hopes and dreams. Ought-is-can-will is the full sequence. When Alexander Pope opined that reality is nothing more than "whatever is, *is* right," he was wrong. Everyone claims to *"know the way it is,"* but in fact they know something more. They also sense *the way things ought to be.* An additional insight is always tagging along *with* our knowledge of what *is*—it's a sense of what *ought* to be. Do you know the Latin word for "with knowledge?"

It's *conscience*, from the Latin *conscientia,* "with knowledge." Simply sequencing *ought plus is* yields the key characteristic that changes the game, human conscience. We don't just know "the way it is." We imagine how life ought to be. *Ought* is a moral term, differentiating right from wrong. We're moral beings. Rats and cats and elephants don't have quite the same faculty.

If your dog pees in my yard, he or she doesn't think twice about it. Dogs and cats are not expected to know better (unless you train them). If, however, you pee in my yard, "Houston, we have a problem." You *ought* to know *better*. Knowing better—or how life ought to be—is the great demarcation between humans and animals.

Human conscience doesn't diminish the nature of animals. Woody Allen was once asked whether he saw some grand design in nature. He said he only saw a large restaurant. When a tiger kills an impala, it's dinner. When a human being kills another human under certain circumstances, it's murder. Animals operate inside nature's rhythms. Human rhythms are informed by our moral responsibilities, our shared sense of *ought*.

Human conscience is different than temperament or personality. Temperament tests, such as the Myers-Briggs Type Indicator, assess our preferences, personality, and how we process information and experiences. As the MBTI appropriately points out, no set of preferences is superior to another. ENTP (extraversion, intuition, thinking, perceiving) is not a better temperament than ISFJ (introversion, sensing, feeling, judging).

Conscience, on the other hand, is not temperament but rather a lens through which we see reality. It is being self-aware—and like any lens, it can bend and flex. Human conscience can warp, blur, blind, or sharpen our perception of reality. You can be an arrogant ENTP or a humble one.

Acting as a lens, conscience lets in the light of knowledge and experience. A lens can afford us a clear picture of reality or it can warp reality. Conscience judges not the *efficiency* of our actions but their *moral quality,* their "goodness" or "badness." Something is *good* when it is fully what it *ought* to be. A good watch does what a watch *ought* to do; it keeps time accurately. A good person does what he or she *ought* to do. Conscience is to the soul what the eyes are to the body. Proper eyesight reveals the proper physical properties of things. A good conscience unveils the proper moral quality of our actions.

"Some of the most poignant examples from great literature paint conscience in this light," writes Thomas Williams. "Think, for instance, of Edgar Allan Poe's 'The Tell-Tale Heart,' in which a guilty conscience gnaws so desperately at the killer that, despite his perfectly executed plan, he ends up turning himself in. Think, too, of Nathaniel Hawthorne's *Scarlet Letter,* or Shakespeare's *Macbeth,* or any number of other classic works where conscience is portrayed especially as a persistent and intransigent reminder of moral guilt." As Shakespeare wrote, "The play's the thing/Wherein I'll catch the conscience of the king."

Or consider Fyodor Dostoevsky's *Crime and Punishment.* Rodion Romanovich Raskolnikov contemplates committing an awful crime, and then does it. Once the deed is done, his conscience begins to grate on him. Dostoevsky's story is rooted in a definition of reality that takes seriously the power of human conscience to restrain or punish immoral behavior.

If conscience is a lens, it is flexible. If it is flexible, it can bend many directions. In fact, the lens of conscience can take four different shapes.

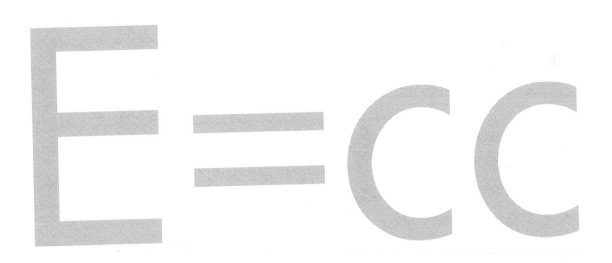

11

THAT LITTLE SPARK OF CELESTIAL FIRE

Labor to keep alive in your breast that little spark of celestial fire called conscience.

—George Washington

When I got hitched to Kathy in 1981, I became aware of my halitosis.

For twenty-seven years, I lived in bliss. My innocent happiness changed when I got married. Kathy was my epiphany. Scientists say we don't smell our own breath odor due to a biological process called *habituation*—we become comfy with our bad breath but can't bear the bad breath of others.

Habituation is an unconscious sensory accommodation helping us sift through new stimuli while keeping the background systems operating. A short time after you got dressed this morning, the stimulus that clothing created disappeared from your nervous system and you became unaware of it. Habituation keeps us sane by desensitizing us—which is *the* occupational hazard of conscience. Habituation means that we can be desensitized to our own conscience.

Human conscience is not readily apparent since it's "an intuitive feeling about the immanent nature of reality," Richard Weaver observed. It's an operating system, like Macintosh OS X. When you use a computer, you're likely unaware of the operating system. People "operate inside" the platform so that they can use programs like Word. In the same way, most of us are unfamiliar with conscience—it's our operating platform. But only one kind of conscience reliably sequences the code. These people expand the moral middle by being obedient to the unenforceable.

One hundred years ago, Lord John Fletcher Moulton, a noted English judge, introduced "the domain of obedience to the unenforceable." He divided human action and society into three domains. If you picture an oval, at one end is the domain of law, "where," Moulton said, "our actions are prescribed by laws binding upon us which must be obeyed." This is the *have-to* part of life. You *have to* obey traffic laws. You *have to* pay your taxes (at least, that *used* to be the case). In our neighborhood, painting the exterior of your home any color requires getting approval from the architectural committee. You *have to*.

At the other end is the domain of free choice, "which," Moulton said, "includes all those actions as to which we claim and enjoy complete freedom." This is the *want-to* part of life. People need some degree of free choice, such as the cereal you ate this morning, the color of clothing you prefer, whether you like veggie pizza or supreme. In our marriage, Kathy and I have *have-to* parts, such as taking out the garbage (my part). We also have *want-to* parts, such as vacationing in Hawaii. Since our tastes are very different, we decided that individual *want-to* days on our Hawaiian vacation were a good idea. Kathy's *want-to* day was meticulously planned down to the minute. My *want-to* day involved renting a Jeep and driving nowhere in particular.

Between these two extremes, Moulton said, is the domain where our actions are not determined by law nor are we free to behave in any way we choose. He considered this to be "the domain of obedience to the unenforceable." This is the "moral middle," the *ought-to* part of life. Moulton's point is simple: the larger the domain of obedience to the unenforceable, the better the society. There are limits to the *want-to* part of life, as we have recently been reminded. We saw the limits in the Merrill Lynch merger with Bank of America in 2008.

At the eleventh hour during tense weekend negotiations, Merrill Lynch's executives decided to enrich themselves and thousands of other employees with up to $5.8 billion in bonuses. It was essentially blackmail. Or greed. Earlier that year, Merrill Lynch CEO John Thain had spent $1.22 million in corporate funds to renovate two conference rooms, a reception area, and his office—including $131,000 for area rugs, a $68,000 antique credenza, guest chairs costing $87,000, a $35,000 commode, and a $1,400 wastebasket. The *want-to* and *have-to* parts of life always try to creep toward the middle of the oval, shrinking the *ought-to* part of life. Bank of America was an example of *want-*

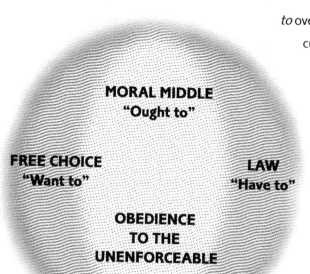

MORAL MIDDLE
"Ought to"

FREE CHOICE
"Want to"

LAW
"Have to"

OBEDIENCE TO THE UNENFORCEABLE

to overrunning the *ought-to*. It's part of a culture that contributed to our economic crisis.

Of course, the cure is often worse than the disease. After capitalists got greedy in the 1980s, Congress passed the Sarbanes-Oxley Act of 2002. Well-meaning but heavy-handed reforms—the *have-to* part of life—drove capital away from New York, making London the world's financial center. In this case, the *have-to* domain crept toward the middle. The solution is not more government oversight. It is expanding the moral middle. Good laws are necessary but they require some wisdom in their administration—along with an understanding that we cannot legislate all human behavior. A better solution is a better definition of reality and assessment of human nature so that people are obedient to what they *ought* to do.

"The real greatness of a nation, its true civilization, is measured by the extent of this land of obedience to the unenforceable," Moulton said. "It measures the extent to which the nation trusts its citizens, and its area testifies to the way they behave in response to that trust." Citizens doing what they *ought to* do are ultimately people of good conscience. This is why starting the sequence with *ought* is critical. "Labor to keep alive in your breast that little spark of celestial fire called conscience," George Washington counsels Americans across the ages. If we don't have individuals and institutions of good conscience, the consequences can be horrific.

In Laurence Rees's book *Auschwitz: A New History,* he notes how the Nazi SS killers were not without tender feelings toward those they slaughtered. He records incidents where the Final Solution upset some of them very much, especially when the Jewish men, women, and children were being prepared for slaughter and began screaming or struggling or fainting. The exercise of corralling humans as though they were animals wore out many SS officers when they tried shooting their victims one by one beside mass graves. That, along with saving on bullets, is why the Nazis built efficient gas chambers, with soundproof walls and nearby crematoria. And it is why they took elaborate steps to mask what they were doing. Their conscience was killing them.

Something that came *with* the knowledge that they were slaughtering millions of Jews struck some Nazis as not quite right. Of course, not every camp worker was troubled. And it's true that few did anything about it. Courage comes from a clear conscience. It's this kind of conscience that can best sequence the code.

In fact, it's this kind of conscience that makes people and organizations self-aware about right and wrong. Conscience is critical to the long-term success of truly innovative companies. An accurate assessment of human nature tells us this. That's because conscience can make companies self-aware.

Ought–Is–Can–Will

12

SELF-AWARE

> Modern man is drinking and drugging himself out of awareness, or he spends
> his time shopping, which is the same thing.
>
> —*Ernest Becker*

Do you know how you *come off?*

"Leaders have to be self-aware. They have to understand their flaws, their own behavior, and the impact they have on others." Wise leaders put self-awareness at the top of any list describing what they look for in colleagues, and why psychologist and author Daniel Goleman argues EQ is more important than IQ. By EQ, he means "emotional intelligence"—the ability to exhibit self-awareness, self-discipline, persistence, and empathy.

Self-awareness is one way the ancients described conscience. Goleman's book was on *The New York Times* bestseller list for more than a year and a half, with some five million copies in print worldwide and it has also been a best seller throughout Europe, Asia, and Latin America, having been translated into nearly 30 languages. Emotional intelligence, Goleman concludes, is a master aptitude, a capacity that profoundly affects all other abilities, either facilitating or interfering with them. That's exactly what the code tells us about human conscience.

Conscience is the uniquely human ability to be self-aware and see the truth about ourselves. Acting as a lens, only a healthy conscience is properly self-aware. This applies just as well to institutions such as business, law, education, and entertainment. They see reality through a corporate conscience. This is a remarkable view of human beings and the institutions they create—*they can be self-aware of their moral responsibilities.* This is why deciphering your company's DNA can be a game changer. Individuals and institutions have the capacity to distinguish between right and wrong. This characteristic of self-awareness distinguishes humans and human endeavors from plant and animal life. This understanding of conscience is, in fact, one of the distinguishing marks of Western culture and civilization.

Michael Novak notes the four fundamental ideas that shaped America—that is, all humans are "endowed with rights by their Creator; *liberty of conscience* [italics mine]; a regulative idea of truth; and historical consciousness"—are "horizon-shaping concepts." This isn't necessarily a religious idea, Novak writes. "Each of these boundary concepts may be articulated in secular terms. It is not necessary to be a believing Jew or Christian in order to hold them in mind or, more exactly, to be held in their grip."

The framers of the U.S. Constitution were held in this grip of conscience. They believed that everyone ought to follow the dictates of conscience. Conscience, however, isn't primarily about religion but about reality. Everyone lives in the code and sees reality through their conscience. Everyone follows the dictates of conscience all the time, not just when it comes to religion. It's how we see reality.

When our son Stephen was a wee lad, it was apparent that his vision was impaired. When Kathy took him to the ophthalmologist, the doctor fitted Stephen with eyeglasses that had lens that looked like the proverbial bottom of a Coke bottle. On the way home, Kathy heard Stephen exclaim in wonder, "Leaves!" Before this time, Stephen perceived trees as big, green, fuzzy lollipops. That was reality in his mind. Correcting the lens helped Stephen see reality correctly. The good news is that as he has grown older, his eyesight has gradually improved—so much so that he hardly needs to wear a corrective lens today.

The little spark of celestial fire sharpens an individual's and an institution's perception of reality or blurs self-awareness. Your company *has* a corporate conscience at this very moment. Conscience can illuminate a path or ignite passions in ways that destroy people. Because conscience is a lens, it can be true or warped. If it's true, people and organizations are trustworthy. They stand a much better chance of achieving their purpose statement. If the corporate conscience is warped, individuals and institutions are in trouble.

Conscience can, in fact, warp in three directions. It can be correctly shaped only one way. Sequencing begins by examining the first way conscience can warp. If the lens bows outward, individuals and institutions become *self-unaware*. They get an inflated sense of their self-worth.

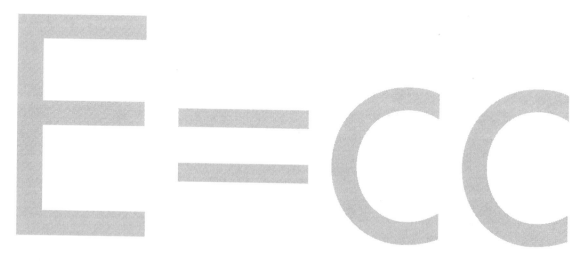

13

INFLATED

Nothing fails like success.

—*Gerald Nachman*

He was doing well until he was doing well.

Kenneth Lay founded the Enron Corporation in 1985 and presided over the company as chairman and CEO until his resignation in 2002, except for a brief period in which Jeffrey Skilling took over in 2001. Enron initially enjoyed great success. Lay was doing well until he was doing well. Then things began to go south and the company collapsed. Yet Lay denied knowledge of Enron's scandalous accounting practices.

Lay and Skilling placed the blame squarely on Enron's chief financial officer, Andrew Fastow. Fastow was found to be complicit and received a six-year sentence in federal prison. Lay was also up to his eyeballs in the scam and was convicted of ten counts of fraud and conspiracy. Lay died, however, before he could be sentenced. In what had been called the granddaddy of all corporate crimes (before the recent economic collapse), the 2006 conviction of Skilling resulted in a prison sentence of twenty-four years.

Kenneth Lay is part of a litany of leaders, including John Thain, Bernard Madoff, Jeffrey Skilling, and others, who saw reality through a lens that was bent outward and magnified their sense of self. They had an inflated conscience.

It could also be called an arrogant or conceited conscience. This self-unawareness causes exceptional people to see themselves as just that—an exception or above the law. They can see the code, but they make too much of themselves. They think too highly of their gifts and talents. They believe they're mostly "damn right." Typically quite successful, they're ultimately prima donnas or egomaniacs. As cultural historian Gerald Nachman reminds us, "Nothing fails like success."

Arrogant people have lost contact with much of reality. But they're savvy, so few notice it. People light up when they enter the room. Over time, they become unaware of themselves because their fawning followers never tell them the truth. Shakespeare described this type of haughty individual in *King Lear*. A powerful man comes to a tragic end because he surrounds himself only with people who flatter him. He slowly but surely banishes the friends who try to tell him the unvarnished truth. Something about success invites suck-ups.

Let's face it; few of us enjoy criticism. Instead we prefer puppies greeting us when we arrive home. We are innately drawn to those who admire us and agree with us, and are inclined to dislike the people who criticize us. Kings, presidents, and CEOs get to decide who surrounds them and what they will hear.

Richard Dortch had a front-row seat for the slow warp outward of a young couple's lens. Jim and Tammy Bakker launched a television program in 1974. Dortch witnessed firsthand the rapid rise and calamitous fall of the *PTL Club.* Afterward, he came face-to-face with these questions: What makes ordinary men and women cross the line and abuse authority? Why do good people, once they are flush with success, often overstep their position of power? Dortch came to appreciate that once people are inflated, they are practically impervious to correction.

For those with this condescending conscience, the code is an opportunity to leverage reality for their own gain and to keep criticism at a distance. You can see this phenomenon in the time it takes an underling to preface a simple observation: "I think—and I could be wrong—that maybe, just maybe, you were, sir, a bit harsh to that company employee . . . but I could be wrong. Maybe . . . I dunno . . . gosh, I guess you're right, boss."

Dutch social psychologist Roos Vonk, who has conducted experiments into how ingratiation works, says, "People in high-powered positions are flattered a lot, so they don't get realistic feedback from others. That happens a lot with politicians because people who support them surround them. They get a very unrealistic image of themselves. They find it difficult to tolerate people who disagree with them, because they don't need to tolerate them, because they have high power—they can always find people who will agree with them."

Conceit or condescension can be hard to see in ourselves. A warped lens might have been the cause of President Reagan's embarrassing problem. He had called on Americans to give and volunteer ("government is not the solution"); yet when Reagan's tax returns were released during his first year in office, they revealed that he gave less than two percent of his income to charity. Blinded by the might.

Pride is the only vice, C. S. Lewis wrote, that we can see plainly in others but are unable to see in ourselves. When the lens of conscience bends outward over time, influential people become insulated. Highly productive organizations become prickly. They view the code of ought-is-can-will—and their place in it—from haughty heights. Individuals and institutions begin to think more highly of themselves than they ought to.

In an era of unprecedented problems, sequencing is serious work. Sequencing any company's DNA requires intelligent and gifted people, but not if they exhibit a pattern of grandiosity, excessive need for admiration and affirmation, entitlement, and lack of empathy toward other individuals (male leaders particularly struggle with underdeveloped empathy, a trait reinforced from early childhood). Inflated individuals and institutions have an unrealistic perception of their accomplishments, their brilliance, and their talent.

At the end of the day, these individuals and institutions cannot properly sequence the code. So what happens when the lens bends inward and individuals and institutions become *self-overaware*?

14

INWARD-BOUND

O coward conscience, how dost thou
afflict me!

—King Richard III, *Richard III*

Have you ever wondered how people get
wrapped around the axle?

A lens can bend outward or inward. Outward
magnifies to a sense of smug arrogance.
Inward goes in the other direction—producing
feelings of inferiority and cowardice. That's
why inward-bound individuals and institutions
often resort to "emotional hostage taking." You
can see it on the international stage as well as
on the interpersonal.

On November 4, 1979, a mob of around five
hundred Iranian students seized the main
U.S. embassy building in Tehran. Tensions had
been building since the 1950s. That was when
the CIA helped the Shah and conservative
elements in Iran remove reformist Prime
Minister Mohammed Mossadegh in what
was widely seen as a coup d'etat. Eight U.S.
presidents had provided the Shah with military
and economic aid. But the Shah's close

Photoillustration / King Richard III, BBC

relationship with the West, along with his opulent Western lifestyle, rankled religious conservatives. His regime was toppled in the Iranian revolution, and the Shah fled the country in January 1979.

The United States exacerbated the damage in October 1979 by admitting the Shah (who was ailing from lymphoma) to the country for medical treatment. This enraged the revolutionary movement, which was not entirely blameless. Islamist fundamentalists had enflamed hatred of the West, exacerbating feelings among students in particular that Iran had been a victim and given a raw deal by the United States. On November 1, 1979, Iran's new institutional leader, the Ayatollah Ruhollah Khomeini, urged his people to demonstrate against U.S. and Israeli interests, encouraging Iranians to vent their feeling of impotence. Students did. They took Americans hostage in the U.S. embassy.

Every person holds power. But not everyone has the same degree of power. Some have more and others have less. People with a healthy conscience can handle this difference. But people with an inward-bound conscience have either mishandled power or have been abused by others' power. When things don't work out as hoped, inward-bound C-level executives often fall back on a compliance form of leadership. They lean too heavily on policies, procedures, rules, and laws, failing to consider the leverage of a good conscience. In the worst case, they curl into a fetal position and play the victim rather than take responsibility and confess their crimes when confronted with reality.

Granted, life is not fair. Individuals with wounded consciences often come from unfair circumstances. It could be from involvement with drugs or alcohol; growing up in a dysfunctional family; pornography, abuse, abandonment; or simply having never received a decent education. But it's not just a case of what's been done to them—it's what they have or haven't done themselves. The Iranians were not entirely innocent. Individuals with inward-bound consciences have trouble 'fessing up to their own sins. They therefore live with unresolved conflicts in society because of unresolved conflicts raging in their souls. The lens then warps. It works the same way with institutions.

Any company can hit a period of poor performance, lose market share, or experience slow decline in profitability. Inward-bound organizations, such as GM, act as though it's the fault of labor unions and government regulations. They have a point—to a point. Labor leaders blame management. Management blames government. They all have a point—to a point. But hardly anyone takes responsibility. Instead, they try to take their perceived opponents hostage.

The result for individuals and institutions is a cruel prison where they step into a cell of their own making, slam the door shut, throw away the keys, and then blame others for their imprisonment. If you fail to feel sorry for them and coddle their captivity, they resent your freedom and blame you for simply pointing out reality. These individuals— and the institutions they create—are cowards. Taking hostages is cowardly. It is manipulation. It is unfair. These kinds of people are kamikazes in companies.

These inward-bound individuals have, in fact, created institutions that have in turn created an entire pop-psychology cottage industry. Moral terms have been trumped by individualized, therapeutic language. "It's true if it feels right," is one way of saying it. Or, "I have to be true to myself." That assumes, or course, that these individuals and institutions see reality correctly.

These inward-bound institutions are easy to spot. They're fluent in Freudian frames to describe their view of reality. It's all about feeling "safe" and being "authentic." The code, with moral categories, sounds threatening. It calls for personal responsibility. It makes people feel "invaded." Reality, however, often blows in like a thunderstorm. Sirens go off unannounced. Insights into our conduct can arrive the same way—unsolicited, yet lifesaving. People and organizations with inward-bound consciences don't see reality this way. As Tommy Lee Jones told Will Smith in *Men in Black*, "They think they've got a pretty good bead on things."

If only that were true.

It's difficult for inward-bound individuals and institutions to sequence the code because *anything* outside their way of seeing things feels threatening. They make you preface, explain, and comfort them before they'll consider any comment that might be construed as critical. When inward-bound individuals feel threatened, they throw conversations off to extremes or twist a discussion into a negotiation about the meaning of terms. Such individuals and institutions suffocate efforts at enjoying obedience to the unenforceable.

But they're not necessarily set in their ways.

A few years back I received a call from Debbie, a senior vice president in a company where I coach colleagues to sequence the code. Debbie described a conversation where one of her people had been performing below expectations. Every attempt to broach the subject was met with deflections and insinuations. Debbie said she suddenly had an epiphany: "You're trying to take me hostage. We don't do that here. It's not the way work ought to be." Debbie told me the woman's eyes got as big as saucers. Taking a time-out, they reconvened the next day. The colleague admitted to operating with a wounded, inward-bound conscience. They began to fix the problem. "This was a game changer," Debbie said.

Inward-bound individuals and institutions can't change the game. They're locked up in a cell. They can't properly sequence a moral code. So what happens when the lens bends too far either way—inward or outward—so that individuals and institutions become *completely unaware?*

15

SHATTERED

> To have people who are well informed but not constrained by conscience
> is, conceivably, the most dangerous outcome of education possible. Indeed,
> it could be argued that ignorance is better than unguided intelligence, for
> the most dangerous people are those who have knowledge without a moral
> framework. It is not the lack of technological information that threatens
> our society; it is the lack of wisdom, and we run the risk today of having our
> discoveries outdistancing our moral compass.
>
> —*Ernest Boyer*

Burgess Meredith was set—until he lost his reading glasses.

Many older baby boomers remember the 1959 *Twilight Zone* episode "Time Enough to Last," where Burgess Meredith finally had the time to read the books he loved—until he stepped on his reading glasses. They were shattered.

The shattered conscience is the result of an arrogant or inward-bound lens bent too far in either direction. When the lens shatters, individuals and institutions no longer see themselves or others. Their lack of self-awareness can be close to 100 percent, completely unaware. This can play out in individuals and institutions that "just don't get it." They can come off like Gene Frenkle, who misplayed the cowbell with Blue Öyster Cult.

> "Okay! Wait! Wait! Stop! Um, Bruce, could you come in here for a minute, please?"
>
> "That . . . that was gonna be a great track. Guys, what's the deal?"
>
> "Uh, are you sure that was sounding okay?"

"I'll be honest . . . fellas, it was sounding great. But . . . I could've used a little more cowbell. So . . . let's take it again . . . and, Gene?"

"Yeah?"

"Really explore the studio space this time."

"You got it, Bruce."

"I mean, really . . . explore the space. I like what I'm hearing. Roll it."

Frenkle was funny. At times the shattered conscience can be funny, even harmless. We all know people who just don't get it. But individuals and institutions seeing reality through a shattered lens can also be deadly. Simon Wiesenthal saw this firsthand.

Wiesenthal was the controversial Nazi hunter who pursued hundreds of war criminals after World War II. Called "deputy for the dead" and "avenging archangel" of the Holocaust, Wiesenthal created a repository of concentration-camp testimonials and dossiers on Nazis after the war that helped bring 1,100 former Nazis to trial. It was, however, a terrifying incident early in the war that aroused Wiesenthal.

In 1939, Ukrainian soldiers rounded up Wiesenthal along with other Jews. Each man stood against a wall, beside a wooden crate that was meant to hold a corpse. An officer would shoot a man in the neck, take a swig of liquor, and then shoot the next man. As the officer approached Wiesenthal, church bells sounded. "Enough!" the officer said. "Evening Mass!"

Wiesenthal's experience brought him face-to-face with this monstrous cruelty. "What I saw for the first time was systematic extermination that had no motive except to kill every Jew, starting with the ones who looked the most dangerous to Hitler," he writes. "And done by people who took real pleasure in killing us."

Wiesenthal was in fact experiencing the consequences of the third type of conscience. When the lens shatters, individuals and institutions can become monsters. Or they embrace various kinds of utopianism. Either way, they certainly cannot properly sequence the code. Wiesenthal witnessed this as an observer at the Nazi war crimes trials held in Nuremberg, Germany. During these trials, Nazi leaders, charged with genocide, mass murder, torture, and other atrocities, repeatedly said, "I was only

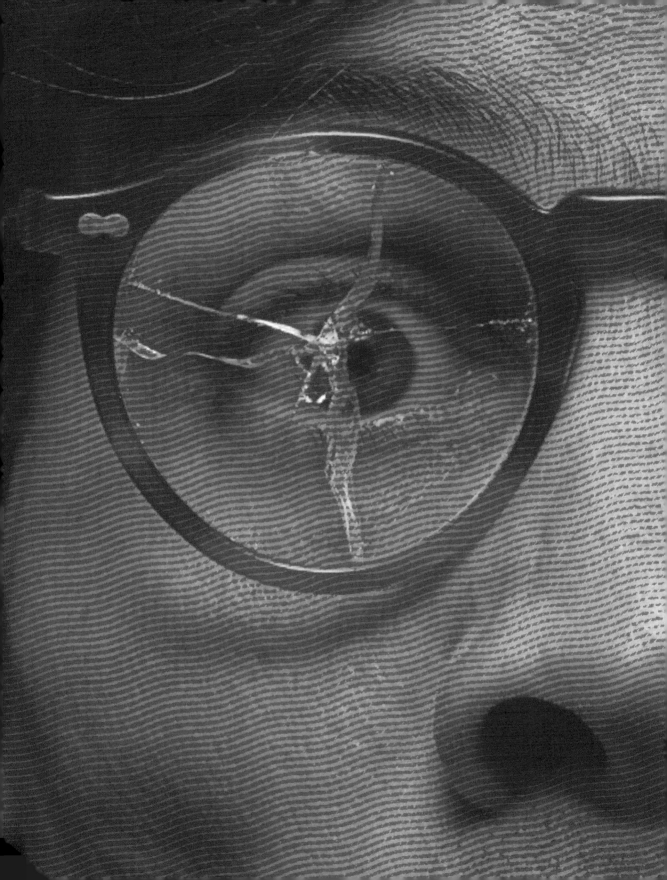

following orders." The statement was invoked so frequently that the argument became known as the Nuremberg Defense.

Wiesenthal and others learned how German physicians planned and enacted the euthanasia program, the systematic killing of those they deemed "unworthy of life." The mentally retarded, the institutionalized mentally ill, and the physically impaired were victims of unconscionable pseudoscientific medical experiments without their consent. They were Jews, Poles, Russians, and Gypsies, who died or were permanently crippled as a result.

This is exactly what Friedrich Nietzsche predicted would happen when people no longer take seriously the idea of a universal code. At the end of the nineteenth century, Nietzsche predicted that the twentieth century would be one of "wars such as have never happened on earth," wars catastrophic beyond all imagining. He said that humankind would limp through the century "on the mere pittance" of the old decaying ideas because we no longer had a shared moral code. If there is no longer any meaning in life or morality, then we are left with *might makes right*.

Individuals and institutions with a shattered lens don't care about the code. They may merely exhibit a failure to conform to social norms, such as Frenkle playing the cowbell with Blue Öyster Cult. Or they may be darker, repeatedly performing acts that are deceitful, irritable, aggressive, or demonic. These individuals and institutions cannot properly sequence the code.

16

CLEAR-EYED

> No Englishman has ever done more to evoke the conscience of the British people and to elevate and ennoble British life.
>
> —*Sir James Mackintosh*, describing the work of the abolitionist William Wilberforce

There's a difference between perfection and being perceptive.

A flexible lens can be properly shaped. This is the clear-eyed conscience. It doesn't make individuals and institutions perfect; it makes them perceptive. People and companies with a healthy conscience still make mistakes. They do things they later regret. But these firms are perceptive about reality and understand how human conscience can change the equation and leverage change. Consider the examples of Peter Peckard, Thomas Clarkson, and William Wilberforce.

Dr. Peter Peckard became vice-chancellor of Cambridge University in 1785. He had repeatedly condemned the slave trade as a "most barbarous and cruel traffick." But Peckard hit on the brilliant idea to put his office to use and "set as a topic for Cambridge's most prestigious Latin essay contest the question *Anne liceat invitos in servitutem dare?*—Is it lawful to make slaves of others against their will?" One of the entrants was a twenty-five-year-old Cambridge student named Thomas Clarkson. His essay was deemed to be the best. He won.

After collecting the prize, Clarkson set off for London. Sitting down to rest by the side of the road at Wades Mill, Clarkson's conscience began to prick him: "it was time for some person to see these calamites to their end." Two years later, on May 22, 1787, the group of abolitionists had grown to twelve determined men who "sat down in the printing shop at 2 George Yard, amid flatbed presses, wooden trays of type, and large sheets of freshly printed book pages, to begin one of the most ambitious and brilliantly organized citizens' movements of all time," Adam Hochschild writes. This group would soon enlist the help of William Wilberforce.

William Wilberforce was born in 1759. He was first elected to Parliament in 1780 at the age of twenty-one, not unusual for those born to the wealthy and landed class at the time. So was his college friend William Pitt. Wilberforce was charming, extroverted, short-tempered, and had a rapier wit that could devastate opponents in parliamentary debate. In 1784, Wilberforce was famously charged by Prime Minister Pitt to "tear the enemy to pieces" in an upcoming debate. He shredded parliamentarian colleague Charles Fox.

After that, Fox bitterly hated him. Wilberforce thought little of it, although he did find his strong temper troubling and fought to curb it. His conscience began to bother him. Two years later, Wilberforce experienced his "great change" and set out to mend his broken relationship with Fox and others whom he had offended. He was also invited to join Clarkson's abolitionist group. Wilberforce did so. He became a man of clear-eyed conscience.

For the next forty years, this group of Clapham colleagues would exemplify what it means to have a clear-eyed conscience. Clarkson searched systematically through every ship in England, port after port, in order to find any sailors who could provide evidence against slavery. (Clarkson found one on the fifty-seventh ship.) He would visit France

"I ought to do . . . as I would be done by." —William Wilberforce

in 1789, believing that the revolution might be a solution for slavery. When it turned bloody, the Clapham group was also bloodied. Clarkson disavowed his former position.

At the age of thirty, on May 12, 1789, Wilberforce made his first parliamentary speech against slavery. Obedience to the dictates of conscience was his principle: "What is there in this life that should make any man contradict the dictates of his conscience, the principles of justice . . . ?" His speech fell on deaf ears. Wilberforce's willingness to seek restoration of broken friendships would ultimately pay dividends. After the death of Pitt in 1806, Fox became part of the administration of Lord George Grenville. Fox and Wilberforce then consulted with each other about legislative strategies to end the slave trade—strategies that were ultimately successful.

Men and women of clear-eyed conscience are game changers. The same holds true for institutions. At the heart of Wilberforce's public philosophy was his deep commitment to the golden rule—"I ought to do," he said, "as I would be done by." That's why the Clapham colleagues once noted they were happy to work with the celebrated orator Richard Sheridan, "whether [he was] drunk or sober."

"A principle on which I have acted for many years," Wilberforce wrote to his son Samuel, "and which I recommend to you early in life, is that of bringing together all men who are like-minded, and may one day combine and concert for the public good."

We need game-changer individuals and institutions like this—using a better definition of reality to serve human flourishing and the common good. This equation can yield great benefits. Or it can produce frightening results.

THREE

SO WHAT?

Sequencing E=cc

When forced to work within
a strict framework, the
imagination is taxed to its
utmost—and will produce its
richest ideas. Given total
freedom the work
is likely to sprawl.

—T. S. Eliot

17

THE HUMAN EQUATION

Now I am become Death, the destroyer of worlds.

—Robert Oppenheimer, after the first atomic bomb test

Albert Einstein was imaginative, but he wasn't perceptive at one point in his life.

A young man once tracked down Einstein and insisted on showing him a manuscript. On the basis of the $E=mc^2$ equation, the man said it would be possible "to use the energy contained within the atom for the production of frightening explosives." Einstein brushed him off, calling the concept foolish. Later in life Einstein recognized the destructive potential in his theory of relativity. He regretted treating the young man's insight so lightly.

So what? What does this have to do with sequencing an organization's DNA?

$E=mc^2$ is Einstein's general theory of relativity. $E=cc$ is the theory of *reality*: the *code times conscience* yields individual and institutional *energy*. It says companies and colleagues are nuclear. As a result, $E=cc$ can yield great benefits or frightening destruction. We have power for good or evil. I was reminded of this not too long ago.

A quiet Monday morning went up in smoke when an old friend called to say that one of his daughters had taken her life. I remembered her high school and college years—she was a bright and thoughtful young woman. In fact, we once spent a day at a bagel shop talking about the human equation. I never learned what she made of our conversation, but her suicide was a sorrowful reminder of the power of this equation.

Because we're hardwired with the code, we think about how work, play, and everything ought to be. We're not animals that only eat, drink, procreate, protect, and defecate. *We're different because we imagine what the world ought to look like.* This is nuclear—for good or evil.

E=cc is the most elementary equation for why we grow companies, amass wealth, raise kids, work out, or run for political office. It's why schools strive to win NCAA sports championships—and why some play by the rules and others cheat. We're not made to simply *get by* but to *get better.* But getting better means we can also get worse—a scary consideration. The human equation tells us why we can head north or south. It contains enormous potential for good or ill.

This deadly potential was poignantly seen in the life and death of Phil Lynott, founder of the Irish rock group Thin Lizzy. In the mid-1970s, Lynott was on top of the world with hits like "The Boys Are Back in Town." Yet with all the money, power, and fame, he sensed a signal pinging his soul for *something more.* The code was telling Lynott that "the way it is"—his wealth and recognition—could be good, but only if he knew *why* he was wealthy. The human equation presses us to figure out how all this stuff *ought to* make the world a better place. It will not let us settle for simply making money.

People can pay attention to the pings or they can squash the signal. Lynott tried to squelch it with drugs, turning to heroin. Close friends tried to help him, including U2 guitarist The Edge. In 1986, Lynott lost the battle. He died of an overdose, a story retold in U2's "Bad."

"The madman is not the man who has lost his reason," wrote G. K. Chesterton. "The madman is the man who has lost everything except his reason." Human beings are the only creatures on earth that commit suicide. Animals don't. Yet suicide is not an irrational act. It's our final, desperate stab at trying to make sense out of life, bending our last shred of reality to how we imagine it *ought to* be. It's a loss of hope in everything *except* reason. It's what happened to my friend's daughter.

The code is reality and is relentlessly rational. This sweet young woman couldn't get around it. Nor could the madman who massacred thirty-two Virginia Tech students in 2007 and then took his own life. What he did was evil, but the pattern he followed was terribly rational. When individuals can't make others bend to their will, their last desperate act is to kill them. Then they kill themselves. Virginia Tech was a horrific act but not entirely irrational.

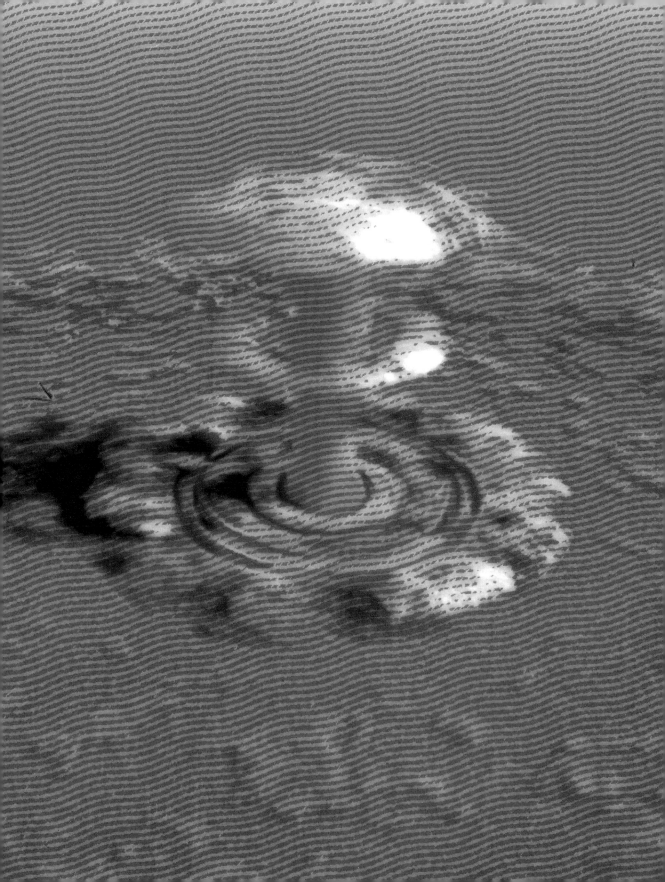

The code is the DNA forming every company or organization. Conscience is how organizations and individuals decipher ought-is-can-will. The *code times conscience* yields human and institutional *energy*. It can create a better culture, if an organization's leadership pays attention to its DNA by properly sequencing it.

Edgar Schein is a Professor of Management at MIT and the author of *Organizational Culture and Leadership*. He argues that one of the primary mechanisms leaders use to create corporate culture is what those leaders systematically pay attention to and measure. In other words, what gets most often *noticed* by leaders in the organization? What gets highlighted more than anything else in your company?

Schein says consistency is more important than motivational pep talks. Pumping people up indicates the tires are leaking. It means the company's culture is not being taken seriously. Leaders then often revert to improving presentation skills rather than acknowledging that employees don't see the culture as connected to reality. Consistently connecting E=cc to as many aspects of work as possible is critical. Take performance reviews.

It is estimated that it takes the average employee six months to recover from an annual performance review. The feedback is often devastating—it raises questions like: "How long have you been thinking this about me?" "Why haven't you told me this earlier?" The most common consequence of a poorly done review is distrust. Properly sequencing E=cc might ensure better reviews that people can receive—ones that take into account human conscience and how it shapes the ability to hear a critique. The way company level leadership administers reviews indicates what they pay the most attention to. They reveal important underlying assumptions about reality.

Here's the bottom line: Only 202 of the 500 biggest companies in America in 1980 were still in existence 20 years later. Long-term innovation is *hard*. To the degree that clear-eyed institutions—and the individuals who shape them—take E=cc seriously and properly act on it, the better they will align with human nature and increase the odds of being truly innovative over the long haul.

This is not reductionism. H_2O reduces water to its essential nature. E=cc reduces reality to its essential nature. E=cc is not formulaic. $E=mc^2$ is a foundational formula.

So is E=cc. It is an accurate assessment of human nature that is critical to the long-term success of truly innovative companies. It tells us that conscience makes or breaks institutions such as firms and families. It produces the culture that keeps companies innovative.

But why so much emphasis on culture? Well, do you own an iPhone?

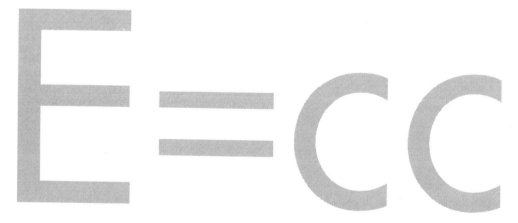

18

WHAT IS CULTURE?

> Culture covers the whole range of human society. It includes not merely art, music, and scholarship, but also such things as our economic and political life, education, the media, marriage, family life, advertising and entertainment. To be a cultural being is, quite simply, to be human.
>
> —*Brian J. Walsh* and *J. Richard Middleton*

I own an iPhone.

If you think about how and why I purchased an iPhone, you can see how *culture* operates. Culture is the governing ideas, images, institutions, and items that shape a society's understanding of reality. Observing culture tells you how reality works and human nature operates. Culture tells you how individuals and institutions change the game. Steve Jobs understands this.

If we're going to change the game, we have to have an accurate assessment of reality and human nature. Culture is created by an endlessly repeating cycle. Let's start with a simple observation about reality: people don't buy *ideas*; they buy *items*. In this case, I bought an iPhone. These products are endorsed by powerful influentials. In this case, Steve Jobs. But influentials like Jobs can only expand their power through an attachment to powerful institutions, such as Apple and AT&T.

These institutions hire other institutions to enhance their ideas and items. In the case of Apple, they retain the services of the advertising firm TBWA\Chiat\Day, who retained the services of U2 to help sell the product. Cool. TBWA\Chiat\Day created attractive advertising that enhanced the image of the iPhone. These attractive images impel people like me to buy a company's products, like the iPhone. This cycle is repeated and a culture is created.

Let's replay that tune.

Culture is *ideas*, or what is known as worldviews. A uniquely American worldview can be summed up this way: "Distance is bad and I ought to be in touch all the time." Where does that come from? On May 24, 1844, Professor Samuel F. B. Morse tapped out a four-word message before a hushed gathering in the chambers of the Supreme Court in Washington, D.C.: "What hath God wrought." It was the first telegram sent over Morse's invention, the telegraph. Americans were beginning to conquer "the first enemy," distance.

Morse grew up in the 19th century, which was characterized by an industrial revolution, a transportation revolution, and a market revolution. In 1817 it took 19 days over backbreaking rutted roads to get from New York City to Cincinnati. But Oxford historian Daniel Walker Howe believes that the 19th century was primarily a "communications revolution." This is because for centuries the most immediate adversary—"the first enemy"—was *distance.* This explains the American assumption that "distance is bad and I ought to be in touch all the time." But culture is more than ideas. It is also *images*, film and art and music and advertising and the stories we tell about "keeping in touch." It is *institutions*, such as

AT&T and Apple that transmit those ideas and make *items*—iPhones being an example—that enable us to keep in touch. Collectively, a matrix such as this one defines what constitutes the good life—*got to have an iPhone or an iPad.*

Culture forms the total and largely invisible matrix of meaning that frames our thinking, guides our actions, and informs what we make and what we long for. Mobile technology is simply one example. Ideas about "being in touch—all the time" are mixed with images in advertising of how cool it is to be in contact with all your friends all the time. Institutions such as the Internet and Apple and phone companies create "cool" items such as phones and Twitter and—presto—you have a culture that doesn't think twice about checking texts and tweets every few minutes. It's a routine ritual. That's culture. It's *institutionalized habits*, like enjoying a warm shower or driving your car—you don't give them a second thought. Institutions shape habits. How?

Neuroscience findings reveal that human beings unconsciously process thousands of signals throughout the day. They come from institutions such as media, our workplaces, music, advertising, neighborhoods, and so forth. Humans however only have the capacity to be conscious of a handful of these impulses at any given moment. We are, in other words, unconscious of most of the cultural influences that impel us. Human beings literally don't have the bandwidth to consciously process all the data simultaneously.

We are, in reality, creatures of habit. Our habits are the results of our desires, and our desires are shaped by cultures. Embedded in these cultures are common sets of assumptions about human nature. These assumptions establish common paths. We operate as enculturated beings, which conveys the picture of a *worn path*. These trails are blazed and paved by institutions like Apple or AT&T. That's why sequencing E=cc institutionally, in your company, will determine if it has the culture to continually innovate.

This assessment of human nature runs against the grain of recent assumptions. Modern management assumes people mostly make *choices*—that the core of our being is our cranium. Therefore, if you train people to think rightly or rationally, they will act rightly and rationally. But prior to the ascension of modern management theory (rooted in a movement called "the Enlightenment" and Descartes' maxim: "I think, therefore I am"), hardly anyone believed that people were fundamentally *thinking* or *worldview* or *believing* or *rationalist* beings. It was assumed that humans are fundamentally *desiring beings*. Dan Ariely splendidly debunks these assumptions in his 2008 book, *Predictably Irrational*.

Ariely shows how real-life decision-making in buying things differs from academic economic models. People make decisions based more on mental frameworks than sound mathematics. For example, American consumers tend to over-value certainty. But this is largely the result of the Enlightenment—and science in general—that promises a world of scientific certainty. Ariely points out how this culture of certainty explains why consumers are willing to buy financial products that otherwise seem to make no sense—such as extended product warranties where the price of the warranty is greater than the expected value of the loss being protected.

Cultures shape desires that shape how people act 95 percent of the time. We are fundamentally desiring beings, oriented primarily by desire, by what we love. These desires are shaped and molded by habit-forming practices in which we participate, the rituals and practices of the workplace, the mall, and the market. In a word, *culture*.

In her last public address at the 175th anniversary of Georgetown University in the fall of 1963, Flannery O'Connor noted: "The things we see, hear, smell, and touch affect us long before we believe anything at all." These experiences are what constitute culture. Cultures shape our imaginations and form our desires. Those desires are how we orient ourselves to reality. Thus, culture is king. It is critical for companies to have the right kind of culture to be continually innovative.

Imagine, for example, how the year 2008 might have turned out if our center financial institutions had taken the E=cc definition of reality seriously and shaped a culture of responsibility. Imagine if most of the culture-shaping financial institutions had stayed out of the subprime market, as T. Rowe Price did. Would the world be a better place with a better definition of reality and human nature that makes business flourish in the proper way? Yes. This, however, is *not* present-day reality.

As a direct result of our economic crisis, *25 percent* of the graduating class of 2009 was unemployed at the end of that calendar year. The code, however, is not the culprit. It is reality. Reality is like gravity, either abide by it or suffer the consequences. You don't break the law of gravity—it breaks you. E=cc is either properly sequenced and companies truly innovate, or it's improperly sequenced (or ignored), and we suffer the consequences. If an arrogant conscience sequences the code, the individuals defining reality will create cultures that contribute to future economic crises. That's reality. If the code is improperly sequenced, real innovation is unlikely. We ignore culture at our peril. This is why corporate culture matters.

Cultures are developed by default or deliberate work. But they *are* developed. Is your company's culture a product of osmosis or organized effort? It is always a combination of being organic and deliberate, yet those organizations that put some thought and effort into it generally build better pathways. They understand that *human conscience* is the key to ensuring the long-term success of innovative companies. If they sequence E=cc, these companies are in fact reframing reality, or how institutions understand human nature.

19

REFRAMING REALITY

> [W]hat's needed are those who can recognize the patterns, and who are highly
> skilled at seeing nuances and the simplicity that may exist in the complexity.
>
> —*Garr Reynolds*

Bill Russell had a high standard for his friends.

The great Boston Celtic center Bill Russell didn't have many friends. But he did enjoy a
lifelong friendship with his coach, Red Auerbach. Russell said Auerbach reminded him of
Albert Einstein. Russell was referring to the famous picture of Einstein standing in front
of a chalkboard filled with dense formulas. Einstein had reduced them to $E=mc^2$. Russell
reduced the complexities of basketball to the essentials.

E=cc takes the complex and reduces it to the essential. This is the promise of sequencing. It
takes the dense threads of daily life and reduces them to the obvious. E=cc reframes reality
as succinctly as possible. It's not a new set of facts. Facts alone don't change anyone. It's a
new frame.

Wait a minute—what do you mean facts don't change anyone?

Facts, as John Adams reminded us, are "stubborn things." The word "fact" comes from
the Latin *factum*, meaning "something has happened." Facts, however, are inert objects.
They just lie there and don't naturally mean anything. You imagine your car is sitting
wherever you left it. But the fact is, you don't know that for certain. You only imagine this
to be true.

We live in our imagination, which always beats facts to the punch. When you're shocked,
it's simply your imagination of what *ought* to be colliding with what *is*. But we usually
don't become aware of imagination until some particular facts don't gibe with our
assumptions.

This is why facts alone do not change us—even facts about good health. The scientifically studied odds are *nine to one*—that's nine to one *against us*—that if a well-informed, trusted authority figure gave us the facts and said we had to make difficult and enduring changes or we would die, *only one in ten would change.* That's why America is not going to solve its overeating problem with more facts. We've got more information on nutrition than ever before! Education alone is not the answer—a new way of *imagining reality* is, which is why Einstein said imagination is more important than knowledge. E=cc is a new way of framing human conscience as the key characteristic for long-term success.

But maybe you believe facts will change people.

Here's a fact: the federal deficit of the United States has ballooned in the last few years. But what does that *mean* when you purchase groceries? Not much. It's a fact, according to the International Monetary Fund, that the public debt of the ten richest countries will rise from 78 percent of gross domestic product in 2007 to 114 percent by 2014. These governments will then owe around $50,000 for every one of their citizens. And the news gets grimmer: the U.S. government's unfunded obligations to give the elderly pensions and health care are equivalent to a debt of $483,000 for every household. *Now* do these deficits begin to mean a little more? Sure they do. It means that lacking the courage of a clear conscience, we're probably not going to reduce these deficits in the near future!

E=cc reframes reality with a simplicity that exists in the complexity. Design consultant Garr Reynolds says we need individuals "who can recognize the patterns, and who are highly skilled at seeing nuances and the simplicity that may exist in the complexity." We then need these individuals to shape the central and periphery institutions that shape human reality and behavior. It can be done.

When Dennis Bakke launched AES Corporation, an international energy distribution company that today has 29,000 employees working in 29 countries, they reduced complexity to four essentials, one being *fun.* By fun, AES assumed people are capable of being responsible. Bakke's thinking was rooted in the ought-is-can-will definition of reality, which begins with an assumption that people are thinking, creative, responsible

Facts alone do not change us
—even facts about good health.

individuals. It blossomed into an organization with no shift superintendents or foremen, no general counsel's office, no finance department, no human resources or personnel department because these functions were "too important to be left to some specialist operation separate from our supervisors."

Under Bakke, AES required every officer to work for one week every year in one of the plants. Every piece of financial information was given to every person in the company. There were no limits as to how much stock any one person could buy in the company. "There is no capital budgeting process as such. There are no salary grades. There are no job descriptions written, by design, and there are no employee handbooks," Bakke added. Treating people as responsible requires an understanding of the role of human conscience in properly defining reality.

Bakke's efforts yielded very good results. But that's not why he did it. Bakke believed it was the right thing to do. Still, a November 1993 report by the investment-banking firm of Kidder, Peabody found that from 1988 to 1992 AES revenues grew at an annual compounded rate of 64 percent. Company earnings during that same time period, the report noted, likewise soared at an annual rate of 136 percent. In 1991, AES's culture was recognized by *Forbes* magazine, along with honoring it as one of "America's fastest-growing companies," an honor AES earned again in 1992 and 1993. It wasn't until AES went public that Bakke's influence began to wane. American corporate culture's systemic commitment to short-term thinking (quarterly reports) and stockholder optimization made his vision difficult to sustain in an economic downturn. It is very telling to note the default operating system an organization uses when confronted with a crisis.

AES is an example of what can happen when institutions zero in on conscience. So how do we begin to sequence the *code times conscience*? Ask yourself which Beatle you most liked—John, Paul, George, or Ringo.

20

CODE TIMES CONSCIENCE

> Perfection is not achieved when there is nothing more to add, but when there is
> nothing left to take away.
>
> —*Antoine de Saint Exupery*

Which one of the Beatles was your favorite?

For those thirty and under, there were four Beatles: John, Paul, George, and Ringo. John Lennon was seventeen when he grabbed a few classmates from Quarry Bank Grammar School in Liverpool and formed the Quarry Men. In the summer of 1957, they were setting up for a performance in a church hall when another member of the band introduced Lennon to Paul McCartney. At that time McCartney was a fifteen-year-old self-taught left-handed guitar player. After the Quarry Men finished their set, McCartney auditioned for the band. Lennon liked him and he joined the band.

The next year, McCartney introduced Lennon to his friend and former classmate George Harrison. The Quarry Men now consisted of Lennon, McCartney, Harrison, piano player Duff Lowe, and drummer Colin Hanton. They broke up, however, in 1959, going in different directions. Harrison joined a group called Johnny and the Moondog, roping in Lennon and McCartney to help him fulfill a contract with Liverpool's Casbah Coffee Club. In 1960, drummer Pete Best joined the group. Over the next eighteen months, they performed in hundreds of clubs and went through a succession of names—Long John and the Beatles, the Silver Beetles, the Beat Brothers—before settling on the Beatles.

In 1962, it was Lennon, McCartney, Harrison, and Best who auditioned for Parlophone Records and producer George Martin at the Abbey Road Studios, where the Beatles would eventually do most of their recording. Martin liked everything about the Beatles except Best. Ringo Starr replaced Best and the rest is history.

So, which one of the Beatles was your favorite?

It's the wrong question, isn't it?

Preferring Lennon or McCartney or Harrison or Starr is neither here nor there. Together, the four produced great music. The code works the same way. It plays in every company like a four-note tune: ought-is-can-will. But one beat is not better than another. There is no right or wrong when it comes to favoring *ought*, *is*, *can*, or *will*. A good organization can have a culture drawn to *ought*. This means it thinks in *patterns*. They're the big-picture companies, imagining how the world *ought* to be. Dennis Bakke spends a great deal of time today thinking about how education *ought* to be. Dennis and his wife, Eileen, founded Imagine Schools in 2004. Taking much of what he learned while heading AES, Bakke is committed to developing schools that make learning joyful by putting teachers and school leaders squarely in charge of the decisions affecting the schools they serve.

There are other organizations drawn to *is*. They think *particulars*. For example, Bloomberg attributes its success to a company culture that creates continually innovative products. The New York-based company focuses on accessing information, reporting it, analyzing it and distributing it to clients—telling them the way the world *is*. These kinds of organizations are realists.

Other institutions are drawn to *can*. They think *pragmatically* about how to get things done. They keep big-picture people from getting carried away in ethereal abstractions and keep realists from the paralysis of over-analysis. Richard Branson of the Virgin companies has created a can-do airline (the same can be said for Southwest). Virgin's latest experimental innovation is airplanes that fly on solar power.

Finally, there are organizations more drawn to what *might* or *will* happen. They help organizations see the *possibilities*. One example is The Global Business Network. They provide tools and expertise, including scenario planning, experiential learning, and other networks of experts to visionary leaders and companies. In the 1980s, GBN advised Royal Dutch/Shell higher-ups to watch out for an unknown Soviet pol named Mikhail Gorbachev. Their strength is focusing on what *will* or *might* happen in the future.

The point is every organization has a "feel"—a culture. Most new hires figure out the feel of an organization by lunchtime of the first day at work. Current employees are largely unaware of the culture because they've become habituated to it. But here's the most important point: It is *the company's leaders* who largely determine *the company's culture*. What makes a healthy culture is healthy leaders properly sequencing E=cc.

The code is reality. Reality is reality. Conscience is *how* the code gets deciphered. The key is multiplying *code times conscience*. To be truly innovative over the long haul, company leaders have to multiply *code times the* right *conscience*. The four beats of the code times the four types of conscience yields 16 different corporate cultures. These cultures are primarily shaped by a company's leaders and become clear when you imagine a four-by-four square matrix. In fact, I recommend you do that right now.

21

THINKING INSIDE THE BOX

People think in frames. To be accepted, the truth must fit people's frames.
—*George Lakoff*

Steve didn't have to take it. They *gave* it to him.

In 1979, Xerox invited Steve Jobs, Bill Gates and other digerati to tour their Palo Alto Research Center. PARC was their "dream lab" in the foothills behind Stanford. They showed their guests three inventions that day. Jobs recalls, "I was so blinded by the first one I didn't even really see the other two. One ... object orienting programming ... I didn't even see that. The other ... was a networked computer system ... using email, etc. I didn't even see that. I was so blinded by the first thing ... the graphical user interface. I thought it was the best thing I'd ever seen in my life." Returning to Apple, Jobs immediately put his people to work on what would become the Macintosh in 1984. Xerox didn't see what they had. They were "just copier heads that just had no clue about a computer or what it could do," Jobs later told PBS. "And so they just grabbed defeat from the greatest victory. Xerox could have owned the entire computer industry today." Apple's innovation still leads the industry. Xerox is out of the computer business and sells printers and copiers.

You might assume that Steve Jobs' success is the result of being able to think outside the box. But the truth is *nobody can think outside the box.* This sounds counterintuitive, doesn't it? Don't business consultants make a ton of money teaching us to "think outside the box?" Of course they do. But that doesn't mean the idea holds water. In fact, it doesn't. Any idea must first fit *inside* a frame (a box or a matrix) in order to make sense. You simply *can't* think outside the box. You can only think *inside* the box.

A host of psychological experiments support this idea. For example, Carnegie Mellon researcher Carey Morewedge and her research team had two groups of volunteers sit in front of the same bowl of M&Ms. One half of the group was told that a packet of M&Ms contained about 3/175 their *weekly* recommended calories. The other half was told the M&Ms contained 3/25 their *daily* allowance (the caloric numbers are roughly equivalent). Yet researchers found "that the two frames of reference made a big difference when it comes to behavior. Volunteers who were asked to think about the weekly number of calories consumed more than twice as many M&M's as those asked to think about the daily number of calories." The difference was the box—our frames of reference for reality. Facts only make sense to us inside a frame of assumptions. "People think in frames," writes George Lakoff. "To be accepted, the truth must fit people's frames. If the facts do not fit a frame, the frame stays and the facts bounce off," writes George Lakoff. You can't think outside the box. You can only think *inside* the box.

Or you can think inside a *better* box. Here's a better box that I'd like you to draw—a new matrix.

Inside this box, draw four vertical columns. Above the box add four labels—one for each of the four columns. From left to right, write OUGHT above the first column, IS above the second, CAN above the third, and WILL above the fourth column. Inside the matrix, add four horizontal rows. Outside the box and down the left hand side, label each row with a type of conscience. From top to bottom, write INFLATED next to the top row, INWARD-BOUND next to the second, SHATTERED next to the third row, and CLEAR-EYED next to the bottom row. Four columns times four rows yields 16 different cultures.

These 16 cultures will overlap and share some similarities, but, as you are about to learn, the 12 cultures produced in the top three rows (INFLATED, INWARD-BOUND, and SHATTERED) are created by leaders whose conscience means they don't take seriously the ought-is-can-will code. That seems a rather large percentage, wouldn't you say? *The New York Times* columnist David Brooks stated the reason well: "For those growing into adulthood during most of the twentieth century, the backdrop of life was a loss of faith in coherent systems of thought and morality."

Translated, most leaders have been trained to discount or debunk any thought of a moral DNA. It's part of American culture. If we are fundamentally enculturated or habitual creatures, then most leaders think little about culture as a matter of habit. For example, in the matrix, leaders with INFLATED consciences shape cultures that assume superiority to any moral code. They *use* culture for personal gain. But no one in the company wakes up in the morning and says: "Let's *use* culture." The conscience of C-level leaders primarily shapes cultures that become habitual.

It works the same way throughout the matrix. For example, therapeutic categories and language ("this is a safe place" and "I feel your pain") have replaced moral categories in much of America. Hence, we have a burgeoning breed of people with INWARD-BOUND consciences—their focus is on their own inner convulsions rather than seeing why culture matters. Corporate leaders with INWARD-BOUND consciences develop therapeutic organizational cultures. They use culture for gain but also for blame. When things don't work out, these organizations find something or someone else to blame— government, stupid workers, or unfair trade practices to name a few. It's a long list.

Finally the loss of faith in coherent systems of thought and morality yields leaders with SHATTERED consciences—they don't give a rip about any code. They couldn't care less about a moral DNA. Corporate leaders with SHATTERED consciences develop companies lacking a soul. It's all about cash. The organizations characterized by these 12 cultures (INFLATED, INWARD-BOUND, and SHATTERED) cannot innovate over the long haul.

As you are about to see, only the final row of company cultures, shaped by leaders with a CLEAR-EYED conscience can innovate over the long haul. *How* they create a corporate culture is what is truly innovative. There is a pattern in their leadership that you can sequence from the code and see in the company. It's the pattern told in the great myths of old. It is universal. This innovative approach to leadership is what leaders with a CLEAR-EYED conscience practice, yielding the kind of cultures that are critical to the long-term success of truly innovative companies.

Here's the good news: I'm giving the box to you.

Culture is most critical to long-term innovation *yet only four cultures inside the box can be innovative over the long haul.* You cannot properly solve a problem if you don't first properly define reality. It begins by asking company leadership how seriously they take their purpose statement.

For example, I've recently been helping a company with a purpose statement that reads: "To restore people, business, and life to the way it ought to be." This company makes dynamic splints that restore range of motion in people's joints. I tell the workers: "Culture largely promotes, permits, or prohibits companies from fulfilling their purpose. To restore people, business, and life to the way it ought to be begins by *defining reality.* What kind of conscience characterizes your company?"

I'm asking you the same question: What kind of conscience characterizes your company? The cultures of 75 percent of today's organizations could not reach a goal such as "restoring people, business, and life to the way it ought to be." They would have to take the code seriously and sequence it properly. Sequencing E=cc will prove this.

Every institution, company, or organization has a conscience. In fact, in this matrix most institutions can be characterized by several of these types of conscience. By multiplying *code* (ought-is-can-will) *times conscience* (inflated, inward-bound, shattered, or clear-eyed) an institution can not only gain insight into human nature but also achieve an accurate assessment of reality. The key is not *which part* of the code your company favors but *which kind of conscience mostly forms your company.* You can't be innovative over the long haul if you're not dealing with reality. Since you can't think outside the box, try sequencing E=cc inside this new box and see whether your company truly has the kind of conscience critical to long-term success at innovation.

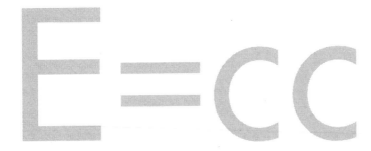

22

ALL THAT . . . AND A BAG OF CHIPS
Human Energy = Ought x Inflated

> Of all tyrannies, a tyranny exercised for the good of its victims may be the most oppressive. It may be better to live under robber barons than under omnipotent moral busybodies. The robber baron's cruelty may sometimes sleep, his cupidity may at some point be satiated; but those who torment us for our own good will torment us without end, for they do so with the approval of their own conscience.
>
> —C. S. Lewis

Is your company all that and a bag of chips?

David and Demi Kiersznowski founded DEMDACO, a design company. They take the code seriously, describing DEMDACO as "pursuing business as it ought to be." They also recognize that *ought* is a moral term. Describing how business ought to be can go straight to the head. When this happens, David says companies start to believe they are "all that and a bag of chips."

That's a great way to describe what happens when you multiply *ought times inflated.* Organizations drawn to *ought* think *patterns.* They're into big pictures, imagining how the world ought to be. That's not the problem. When, however, you think you know how things ought to be, you get arrogant institutions that think they know what's best for everyone. They're superior to the code. They're all that and a bag of chips. Do you work in such a place?

My father believed he did for many years. After earning his undergraduate degree, my father took a teaching position at General Motors Institute in Flint, Michigan. Back then it was assumed that if GM sneezed, America caught a cold. But my father didn't take this as a complete compliment. He feared it would yield a haughty sense of smug superiority. He began to notice that the fit and finish of some GM cars was slipping. GM smugly assumed consumers would be loyal, no matter what. It's what American consumers *ought* to purchase.

The height of arrogance might have been in the 1970s, when GM divined that customers demanded diesels. GM simply slapped diesel parts on Oldsmobile 350 V-8 internal combustion engines. The head design and head bolts were not able to withstand the higher cylinder pressures and temperatures of diesel combustion. This led to catastrophic failure of pistons, cylinder heads, and even cylinder walls. Was GM's corporate culture the product of multiplying *ought times inflated?*

Does multiplying *ought times inflated* account for the struggles of U.S. legacy airlines? I fly Southwest Airlines in the States, but recently I had to book a flight to Boston on one of the legacy lines. When I had to make a change in my flight schedule, the customer service agent told me that there would be a $150 charge to rebook the $149 flight. When I mentioned that it'd be cheaper to simply place the $149 in an account for a future flight, she informed me that they don't do that—there are no accounts that hold customer funds. When I replied that Southwest doesn't charge and would simply hold the funds—at no charge—she informed me that they are not Southwest. Exactly... and they don't have the profits of Southwest, either.

Has an institutional ethos of *ought times inflated* yielded the corporate culture of the legacy airlines? Flying was cool at one time. All that and a bag of chips can be the bane of beautiful institutions. Smart people create smart organizations that begin to assume they know what's best for everyone.

Does *ought times inflated* occasionally yield a smug sense of exceptionalism in Washington, D.C.? Does this sequence yield the slightly embarrassing episodes when a handful of Obama appointees failed to pay all their taxes?

And what about the culture of higher education today? In 2002, the American Enterprise Institute published a report where researchers found a uniformity of political allegiance in major university faculties. Most colleges and universities tout diversity, yet there's no such animal as political diversity among the faculty. Is this a case of institutions—and those who lead them—believing they are all that and a bag of chips?

The researchers visited 21 colleges or universities, including such institutions as Cornell, Brown, Harvard, and Stanford. According to *The Wall Street Journal,* they looked at party registration for faculty members in various academic disciplines. Researchers categorized Republican or Libertarian on the Right, and Democrat, Green, or the like on the Left. At Cornell, they found one English Department member in a party of the Right as opposed to 35 registered on the Left. In the History Department they found no one registered on the Right, but 29 on the Left.

Does it seem a bit smug to tout diversity when there is a wider and freer cross-section of opinion in the aisles of any grocery store or on a city bus than there is now at our colleges and universities? Is it a mark of institutions believing they are all that and a bag of chips when they ignore such incongruities? "That this lack of faculty diversity eludes university administrators is especially interesting given the totality of their efforts to reorder all other aspects of campus life based on that principle," the *Journal* writes.

Properly sequencing reality raises hard questions, especially for financially successful companies or individuals hitting their numbers. For example, do financial incentives lower the level of performance in workers and caring about corporate culture? Alfie Kohn cites research indicating that tangible rewards can actually lower the level of intrinsic interest in a task. Getting people to be creative and take corporate culture seriously is then undercut by a corporate culture of financial rewards that "encourages people to focus narrowly on a task, to do it as quickly as possible, and to take few risks," Kohn notes. Extrinsic rewards can erode intrinsic interest. In other words, expanding the moral middle through conscience cannot be bought. Bonuses might in fact undercut a healthy culture. A more accurate assessment of human and institutional nature indicates that people "are more interested when their curiosity is aroused—when discrepancies exist between what they thought was true and what they've just encountered," Kohn writes. Sounds like the code, doesn't it?

In his book *Wealth Addiction*, author and sociologist Philip Slater notes that: "Getting people to chase money… produces nothing except people chasing money." Using money as a motivator leads to a progressive degradation in the quality of everything produced," including culture. Sequencing *ought times inflated* raises hard questions about the culture of your workplace.

Multiplying *ought times inflated* yields institutions that can sound self-righteous, haughty, patronizing, and pompous. Does this account for some of the current configuration of the business, political, and educational culture? We can't properly sequence E=cc if we don't first accurately define reality.

No organization is perfect. Every organization has preferences. Institutions with good returns, highly educated people, or a highly incentivized workforce can easily become all that and a bag of chips. This is why 75 percent of the time, the problem is not the problem. The problem is instead corporate conscience, or, in this case, the product of multiplying *ought times inflated*. Companies characterized by "all that and a bag of chips" are unlikely to enjoy long-term success at being truly innovative.

23

IT IS WHAT IT IS
Human Energy = Is x Inflated

> If there is a dividing line between liberty and license, it is where freedom of speech is no longer respected as a procedure of the truth.
>
> —*Walter Lippmann*

It is what it is—and that's it.

In 1961, Philip Pearlstein began to paint pictures of nude people. But Pearlstein stripped the nude of almost all its customary associations—beauty, narrative, and symbol. As *The New York Times* noted, "the traditional justifications for nudity in painting were gone, leaving only the bare fact of the naked human body." Art critic Frank Stella said of Pearlstein's paintings, "What you see is what you see." The *Times* wrote, "It is what it is."

That's a great way to describe what happens when you multiply *is times inflated*. A company drawn to *is* thinks *particulars*. It's the kind of organization that keeps our feet on the ground. That's not the problem. When, however, you multiply *is times inflated*, we get institutions that only see particles—there is no grand story or narrative or code. They are superior to the code. Life is what it is. Do you know of such places?

Does this explain much of modern art? Does *is times inflated* yield such works as *Piss Christ* by Andres Serrano, a photograph of a crucifix immersed in his own urine? Many art critics praised his works as expressing concern about the Catholic Church's position on many contemporary issues or as simply exercising his freedom of expression. But when Catholics offered criticism, suggesting that some of Serrano's pieces take inappropriate liberties, they're rebutted. It is what it is.

Why do I get a sense that so many of today's art institutions arrogantly shut out serious considerations of what art ought to be? I have a friend in Shanghai. She was listening to one of the city's leading art critics describing the rapturous beauty embedded in a blank canvas. No kidding—the canvas was blank. Nothing there. It is what it is. When my friend suggested, ever so humbly, that perhaps this painting does not quite capture what art ought to be, people stared at her as if she were a Martian.

Is this the result of *is times inflated*?

Isn't art—in the best sense—supposed to tell the truth about the human condition? Shouldn't it be about truth and beauty? Is it only about freedom of speech?

"If there is a dividing line between liberty and license," Walter Lippmann noted, "it is where freedom of speech is no longer respected as a procedure of the truth and becomes the unrestricted right to exploit the ignorance, and to incite the passions, of the people. Then freedom is such a hullabaloo of sophistry, propaganda, special pleading, lobbying, and salesmanship that it is difficult to remember why freedom of speech is worth the pain and trouble of defending it."

Does sequencing *is times inflated* also reflect much of today's institutions of education?

Does *is times inflated*, for example, explain why so many elite colleges and universities have become institutions of "excellence without a soul," according to former Harvard College dean Harry Lewis? He says Harvard "articulates no ideals of what it means to be a good person, as opposed to an evil person." It is what it is. Lewis says the decline began with the 1825 vote of the Harvard Board of Overseers. This "marked the moment when depth and specialized learning began to ascend in university culture over breadth and the interconnection of knowledge." The point of a college education became about making a living rather than living well. Is this the result of *is times inflated*?

Lewis believes that "the scholars who make the greatest contributions are those whose depth of knowledge is matched by their breadth of understanding, those able to draw on interesting things that were learned even though they seemed irrelevant. Such breadth is exactly what makes professors inspiring and wise mentors to the young. Sadly, this is given scant value in today's colleges." Why?

Could it be that students recognize that *ought* is about right and wrong, and educational

institutions no longer teach right and wrong? Life is what it is. Does *is times inflated* explain why, according to Lewis, "Universities affect horror when students attend college in the hope of becoming financially successful, but they offer students neither a coherent view of the point of a college education nor any guidance on how they might discover for themselves some larger purpose in life"? Has a university degree become merely a passport to privilege?

Since the 1960s, UCLA's Higher Education Research Institute has conducted the nation's longest-running and most comprehensive assessment of the attitudes and plans of the nation's students entering undergraduate classes. Mapping the priorities of tens of thousands of incoming freshmen, they discovered a dramatic change in students' desires to "develop a meaningful philosophy of life." Only 39.3 percent of students viewed it as an important life goal in 2003, compared to 40.6 percent in 2002 and a high of 85.8 percent in 1967. Of course, students didn't have a uniting cause such as the Vietnam War, and this might be a factor.

Multiplying *is times inflated* might yield what Sydney Finkelstein calls "Zombie Businesses." They are companies and organizations that have created "insulated cultures that systematically exclude any information that could contradict its reigning picture of reality." It is what it is—damn it. For six years, Finkelstein's research team at Dartmouth's Tuck School of Business studied business breakdowns, including Motorola's failure to shift from analog to digital cell phones, Rubbermaid's ruinous battle of wills with Wal-Mart, and the implosion of advertising icon Saatchi & Saatchi.

Interviewing 197 top executives, Finkelstein's team discovered that when a company begins to hit the ball out of the park, their perception of reality warps. Enron for example had this sign inside the entrance to its corporate headquarters: "The world's best energy company." Later, it was changed to read, "The world's best company." Finkelstein writes that "this inaccurate picture of reality" is kept in place by a relentlessly positive attitude that shuts out critical information from outside the company. Ra-ra eclipses realism. They lose track of the way it *really* is.

"It is what it is" is not resigning your company to reality. It's an arrogant "up yours" that my company doesn't need to change all that much. *Is times inflated* yields companies

Develop people who can see patterns, not just particles.

that are self-righteous yet also "stuck." They can't innovate. Much of the current configuration of business, the arts, and education is stuck. We can't properly sequence E=cc if we don't first accurately define reality.

Properly sequencing reality demands asking hard questions. Is your company arrogant? We can't solve a problem if we don't begin with reality. No organization is perfect. Every organization has preferences. Institutions with highly artistic and intelligent individuals can easily shrug off their critics with, "It is what it is." They can't innovate.

This is why 75 percent of the time, the problem is not the problem. The problem is corporate conscience, or, in this case, the product of multiplying *is times inflated*. Companies characterized by "it is what it is" are unlikely to enjoy long-term success at being truly innovative.

24

COCKSURE
Human Energy = Can x Inflated

Before the Second World War I believed in the perfectibility of social man . . .
but after the war I did not because I was unable to. I had discovered what one
man could do to another. I must say that anyone who moved through those
years without understanding that man produces evil as a bee produces honey,
must have been blind or wrong in the head . . . I believed then, that man was
sick—not exceptional man, but average man. I believed that the condition of
man was to be a morally diseased creation and that the best job I could do
at the time was to trace the connection between his diseased nature and the
international mess he gets himself into.

—*William Golding*

Can-do people sure can be cocksure.

Jimmy Cayne ran Bear Stearns—right into the ground. An avid bridge player, Cayne
believed that he could objectively analyze his own strengths and weaknesses, as well as
his opponent's. "Then we have some success," Malcolm Gladwell writes, "and begin to
feel surer of ourselves. Finally, we get on the top of our game and succumb to the trap
of thinking that there's nothing we can't master." General Douglas MacArthur comes to
mind: "The hunger for praise that led him on some occasions to claim or accept credit for
deeds he had not performed, or to disclaim responsibility for mistakes that were clearly
his own; the love of the limelight that continually prompted him to pose before the
public as the actual commander on the spot . . . his tendency to cultivate the isolation
that genius seems to require, until it became a sort of insulation . . . that deprived him

of the critical comment and objective appraisals a commander needs . . . the headstrong quality . . . that sometimes led him to persist in a cause in defiance of all logic; [and] a faith in his own judgment that created an aura of infallibility and that finally led him close to insubordination," General Matthew Ridgeway wrote.

Cocksure is a great way to describe what happens when you multiply *can times inflated*. Organizations drawn to *can* think *pragmatically*. They keep big-picture people and realists from getting stuck in abstractions or analysis. That's not the problem. When you multiply *can times inflated*, however, you get institutions that are cocksure. They are superior to the code. Do you work in such a place?

Did *can times inflated* yield the spectacular rise of Bear Stearns? Founded in 1923, Bear Stearns was a bit player to its more blue-chip counterparts like Morgan Stanley and Goldman Sachs. By 2003, however, Cayne had turned the company into a player. "We were hitting on all 99 cylinders," he told *The New York Times*, "so you have to ask yourself, What can we do better?" Cayne decided to borrow and bluff his way to the top. Even after Bear Stearns collapsed, Cayne reported that he received congratulatory accolades—all in one day—from the president's advisory group, the retail sales force on the Web, and a partners' meeting. "Until the very end, he evidently saw the world that he wanted to see," Gladwell concludes.

Does *can times inflated* yield cocksure institutions such as Enron? In 1998, as Enron Corporation was collapsing, the company designed and maintained a phony trading room on the sixth floor of their downtown Houston headquarters. It was designed to impress Wall Street analysts when they visited. Enron executives rushed about 75 employees, including secretaries and actual sales representatives, down to the phony trading room and told them to act as if they were trying to sell energy contracts to businesses over the phone. "It was an elaborate Hollywood production that we went through every year when the analysts were going to be there to impress them to make our stock go up," former employee Carol Elkin said. It was all an act. The people on the phones were talking to each other. "It was absurd that we were doing this," Elkin added.

"Absurd" is a telling word. It means *senseless*. Absurdity treats morality as wink-wink, nod-nod. There is no up or down, no right or wrong. In business, profits become preeminent. Any purpose beyond that is nice but not necessary for the business to flourish.

In reality, corporate malfeasance is *obscene*. "Obscene" means "without story." All good cultures are based on a code—ought-is-can-will—that reads like a story. Behaviors deviating from this code were once considered obscene. People object to obscenity, because it has a moral dimension, a storied "ought." They don't object to absurdity, because it accepts reality "as it is" without purpose or a moral framework. That's why no one spoke out at Enron. The business of business was making money.

Institutions promote, permit, or prohibit individual behavior. In the cases of Bear Stearns and Enron, did *can times inflated* yield institutions that saw themselves as above the law? Did they create individuals who complied rather than complained? Did overlapping institutions, in fact, produce moral muteness?

Frederick Bird and James Waters have observed "moral muteness" in business. Even when business managers are acting for moral reasons, they fear jeopardizing their careers and instead talk about what's "practical," "good for the organization," and making "economic good sense." Moral terms like "we *ought* to do this" are viewed as illegitimate or awkward.

Researchers Joseph Badaracco and Allen Webb say business people learn to be mute while in college. A decade ago, they interviewed Harvard MBA graduates about what they see in modern corporate culture. One student, representative of the majority of graduates, commented, "First, performance is what really counts, so make your numbers. Second, be loyal and show that you're a team player. Third, don't break the law. Fourth, don't overinvest in ethical behavior."

An Aspen Institute study yielded similar results. A survey of about 2,000 graduates of the top 13 business schools found that B-school education not only fails to improve the moral character of the students, it actually weakens it. The study examined student attitudes three times while they were working toward their MBAs: upon entering, at the end of the first year, and upon graduating. Those who believed that maximizing shareholder values was the prime responsibility of a corporation increased from 68 percent upon entrance to 82 percent by the end of the first year. The survey indicated that students gained confidence in things like controlling costs but lost confidence in a moral code. This is a case where expediency is the quiet enemy of conscience. Practicality can be very seductive.

The arrogance of expediency becomes clearer when you apply it to a marriage. You can make a baby in minutes. That's the expedient way. But you can't make love that quickly. Corporate cultures, like a marriage culture, generally suffer when measured under the rubric of expediency.

This is why the student's loss of confidence in a moral code is exactly what we should expect. Philip Rieff said we live in an unprecedented age, a "self-dismantling" of our historic culture rooted in a moral order. A university education has long been part of "a vast self-knowledge industry that is the exact equivalent of invincible ignorance," Rieff said. Students are taught a definition of reality that makes an absolute distinction between facts and values. *Facts* are the province of science and business while *values* are the province of morality. Facts are propositions—what *is* and *can* be done. Values are preferences—what *ought* to be. Fact language includes economics. Values language includes ethics. Students graduate with an unshakable faith that moral language has no place in the workplace.

Does this account for no Enron manager objecting: "*We should not be doing this!*" Was Enron's moral muteness merely a precursor to WorldCom, Bear Stearns, Countrywide Financial, Broadcom, Lehman Brothers, and AIG? Does *can times inflated* yield these results?

Properly sequencing reality means facing reality. Does *can times inflated* characterize your workplace? If so, you can see why 75 percent of the time the problem is not the problem. The problem is corporate conscience, or, in this case, the product of multiplying *can times inflated*. Companies characterized as cocksure are unlikely to enjoy long-term success at being truly innovative.

25

PRESUMPTUOUS
Human Energy = Will x Inflated

> There is not the slightest indication that nuclear energy will ever be obtainable. It would mean that the atom would have to be shattered at will.
>
> —*Albert Einstein*

Einstein couldn't see over the horizon. That's because the world isn't flat. It's curved.

A curved world is reality. That's why it's difficult to see the future according to David M. Smick, author of *The World Is Curved*. For example, Smick says our current economic crisis is rooted in the 1998 collapse of the hedge fund Long-Term Capital Management. Global banks presumptuously tightened the regulations on hedge funds but loosened them on their own trading desks, freeing bankers from the economic consequences of risk. By creating off-balance-sheet vehicles such as mortgage-backed securities, "the new bankers engaged in risk *dispersion*, thinking they had discovered 'riskless risks.' " They thought they saw the future. It was presumption. In reality, no one sees the future.

Presumption is *will times inflated*. Institutions run by intelligent and gifted individuals often assume they see the future. It's the conscience of conceited conjecture. It sees itself as superior to the code. It's a hubris that led *The New York Times* to predict in 1936: "A rocket will never be able to leave the Earth's atmosphere."

Does deciphering *will times inflated* account for our recent spate of greedy capitalists? In hindsight, it was presumptuous. At that time, subprime mortgages and leveraged finances held the promise of a feathered nest and a big nest egg. Yet, as Wendell Berry warns, when the value of a house is in its resale value, it's no longer a home.

"The bomb will never go off," predicted Admiral William Leahy in 1945, as a member

of U.S. Atomic Bomb Project. "I speak as an expert in explosives." In 1957, a Senate subcommittee predicted that by 1985 the average workweek would be down to 22 hours and people would be retiring at the age of 38. How's that working out? Sound a bit presumptuous? It certainly wasn't innovative.

This isn't a tirade against planning. It's a caution against presumption, based in a uniquely American trait. "Americans live now (and always have) in the future tense," *The New York Times* columnist David Brooks writes. As Richard Hofstadter once wryly remarked, "The United States was the only country in the world that began with perfection and aspired to progress."

Americans love to hear institutional leaders promise what we all know they cannot pull off, given the current equations. It's ignorance passing itself off as innovation. But how will politicians make Congress work inside the present reality of caustic polarities? How will Washington find a solution for health care that doesn't bankrupt future generations? As long as Americans feel entitled to eat whenever they want to, whatever they want to, and as much as they desire—and also feel entitled to affordable, universal health care for whatever will invariably ail them—there is no solution. It's like saying every individual is entitled to drive as he or she wishes, and then promise to provide affordable auto insurance.

We need a new equation that doesn't make presumptuous promises. E=cc is it, since it understands the reality of institutions and individual behavior and how hard it is to change. E=cc doesn't make outlandish promises for a quick fix.

Presumptuousness is pervasive in business literature as well. Several years ago, *Fast Company* published an article called "In Praise of the Purple Cow." The author pointed out that brown cows are boring. But if you saw a purple cow in a field, you would notice it. Workers should be purple cows. Business consultants hailed this supposedly amazing insight: "Read this article! It will change your life! Be the purple cow!" Of course, a few years before, everyone was moving his or her cheese. This isn't innovation.

"There will never be a bigger plane built," predicted a Boeing engineer after the first flight of the 247, a twin-engine plane that held ten people. In 1957, Sir Harold Spencer Jones, astronomer royal of England, said, "Space travel is bunk." Two weeks later, the Soviet *Sputnik* orbited the Earth. Presumption is a killer.

Tris Speaker, baseball hall of famer, predicted in 1919 that taking the best left-handed pitcher in baseball and converting him into a right fielder "is one of the dumbest things I ever heard." He was talking about Babe Ruth. In 1932, Einstein confidently predicted: "There is not the slightest indication that nuclear energy will ever be obtainable. It would mean that the atom would have to be shattered at will." It's usually highly intelligent people, those whose lens is most likely bent outward, who make presumptuous predictions. When they run institutions, the fallout can be spread much wider. "That virus is a pussycat," noted Dr. Peter Duesberg in 1988. Duesberg was a professor of molecular biology at U.C. Berkeley. He was describing HIV. "If excessive smoking actually plays a role in the production of lung cancer, it seems to be a minor one," W. C. Hueper noted in 1954. He worked with the National Cancer Institute.

Presumption is assuming the housing market will never stop growing—and selling mortgages to buyers who would never qualify for a loan if sanity ruled. Insanity is simply sequencing the same old equations—greed, arrogant forecasting, and presumption—and hoping for a different outcome. Smick believes that the policy world needs a "big-think" financial doctrine. Sequencing E=cc is a better solution, since it correctly assesses the nature of institutional and individual behavior and how hard it is to change. E=cc doesn't make presumptuous promises for a quick fix. Making culture is a long-term, arduous task that is never completed.

Presumptuousness is often born of distance. Too many leaders try to motivate from the corner office or with bonuses. It's leading by laptop. These men and women create clever videos and motivational messages. Creating a culture of clear-eyed conscience on the other hand requires leaders to get close to the staff, customers, and stakeholders. They find ways to create mediums of feedback with the awareness that all mediums, such as suggestion boxes, wear out over time. Leaders have to be creative without being corny. They have to make prognostications without being presumptuous. Real leadership walks the shop floor.

Does your workplace have an air of presumptuousness? If so, you can see why

75 percent of the time, the problem is not the problem. The problem is corporate conscience, or, in this case, the product of multiplying *will times inflated.* Companies characterized as presumptuous are unlikely to enjoy long-term success at being truly innovative.

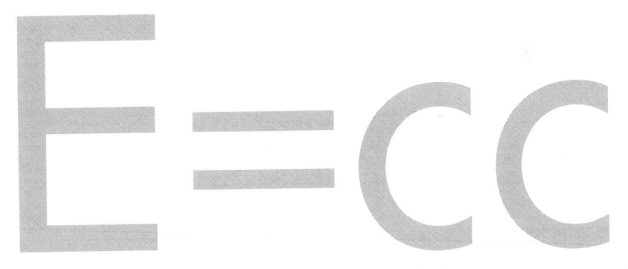

26

ENTITLED

Human Energy = Ought x Inward-Bound

> We believe that each man must find the truth that is right for him.
>
> Reality will adapt accordingly.
>
> The universe will readjust.
>
> History will alter.
>
> We believe that there is no absolute truth
>
> excepting the truth that there is no absolute truth.
>
> —*Steve Turner,* from "Creed"

Sixty percent rated themselves at the top 10 percent.

In 2007, 82 percent of American drivers rated themselves among the top 30 percent in terms of safety. Judging from what we see on the streets, this is a major disconnection from reality. In one College Board survey of almost a million high-school students, only two percent rated themselves below average in leadership ability. When it came to getting along with others, zero percent (that's not a typo) rated themselves below average.

Welcome to the triumph of the therapeutic. Individuals and institutions drawn to *ought* think *patterns*—big pictures describing how the world ought to be. But across the second row of the matrix, the inward-bound conscience takes a therapeutic tack in navigating reality. When you multiply *ought times inward-bound*, we get a pattern of entitlement. Do we see this in sports leagues, educational institutions, and how our culture views retirement?

Narcissus by Michelangelo Merisi da Caravaggio (1594-1596)

"America is a culture of narcissism," wrote Christopher Lasch in his 1979 book, *The Culture of Narcissism*. Narcissism is an ancient idea dating back to Greek mythology. According to legend, Narcissus was a beautiful Grecian youth who fell madly in love with his reflection in a pool of water. Unable to avert his eyes from the image of his own face, Narcissus knelt too close to the water, fell in, and drowned. Are American youth drowning in narcissism?

Alan Chhabra is a thirty-one-year-old who works at Egenera, a computer-server manufacturer. But he's not your typical employee. "I have no problem knocking on the door and walking into the CEO's office or the CTO's office on a whim—interrupting their schedule—and saying, 'I need to talk to you.' " Chhabra is part of the so-called entitlement generation, writes Jake Halpern, the author of *Fame Junkies*. "They are smart, brash, even arrogant, and endowed with a commanding sense of entitlement."

Halpern suggests that the entitlement generation includes virtually everyone born after 1970—a conclusion that Jean Twenge, a psychology professor at San Diego State University, shares. According to Twenge, these young people were raised on a daily regimen of praise and flattery from their baby-boomer parents and from teachers who embraced a self-esteem-boosting curriculum. Is this the result of *ought times inward-bound?* Do youth and parents believe that kids deserve a break?

Does this equation explain our modern sports leagues where players receive trophies for simply showing up? Are these constant reinforcements largely responsible for those young co-workers who are out of touch with reality? At the University of South Alabama, for example, psychology professor Joshua Foster has assessed this disconnect from reality by using findings from the Narcissistic Personality Inventory (NPI). The NPI asks subjects to rate the accuracy of various narcissistic statements, such as "I can live my life any way I want to" and "If I ruled the world, it would be a better place." Does *ought times inward-bound* explain why no group *anywhere in the world* has scored higher than the American teenager? Does it account for Twenge's observation that narcissism and entitlement also appear to be reaching new highs among American college students?

In colleges and universities, grades started to shoot up nationwide in the 1960s, leveled off in the 1970s, and then started rising again in the 1980s, according to Stuart Rojstaczer, a former professor of geophysics at Duke University. The author of *Gone for Good: Tales of University Life After the Golden Age* and creator of gradeinflation.com, Rojstaczer writes that "grades continue to go up regardless of the quality of education." At elite Brown University, for example, two-thirds of all letter grades given are now A's.

Grade inflation couldn't happen without overlapping networks of institutions that promote a therapeutic approach to reality. Seen as a passport to privilege, college preparatory institutions promote self-esteem and high GPAs as access to upper-echelon colleges and universities. Does *ought times inward-bound* yield colleges that give students a wide berth with inflated grades?

And does this equation account for the sense of entitlement among senior citizens? Most of us know that Social Security trustees project a Social Security shortfall to the tune of $3.7 trillion over the next seventy-five years. While the problem is vexing, the solution strategies are simple—increase the supply of money to pay the bills or decrease the demand for benefits.

Or we could ask: Is retirement what we ought to do? Inward-bound institutions might find this troubling to tackle, yet for most of human history, that's the way the real world worked. Until the 20th century, people did not retire. They worked and then they died. In fact, work was viewed as a central feature of *every* stage of life. Though specific working responsibilities often changed with each stage of life, they remained until their last days. Work, after all, was a family affair. People worked to eat and to care for their families. In the process, they felt productive and stayed connected with each other.

Retirement, as a stage of life, is a development of the second half of the 20th century. It is true that Prussian chancellor Otto von Bismarck invented social security in the 1880s, when he set the retirement age at 65. However, since the average life expectancy was 45, this new social invention was not relevant to the lives of most people. As Michael Novak observed, "When Bismarck promised his generals a guaranteed pension after age 65, he knew that few would actually live longer than that."

In the United States, President Franklin Roosevelt signed the Social Security Act into law on August 14, 1935. The new legislation created a social-insurance program designed to pay retired workers a continuing income after age 65. At that time, the average life expectancy was 61. So Roosevelt's Social Security, like Bismarck's, was more of a safety net for those who made it past 65. It was not designed to fund a new lifestyle for golden years of perpetual leisure and relaxation for large numbers of people.

You can see how these programs institutionalized a sense of entitlement. For the past five decades, leisure-oriented golden years have emerged as the archetype for retirement, with seniors golfing, taking cruises, and eating out. The essence is a long, relaxing vacation at the end of a busy life of sweat and toil. It has even been incorporated into the American dream. The result is a system in crisis as a consequence of the collision of demographic realities (life expectancies nearly doubling in the 20th century—from 47 years to nearly 80 today) with fiscal realities (from more than 30 working people for each one retired to fewer than three today).

The problem with people laboring with an inward-bound conscience is they are stricter in their moral judgment of others but are more lenient about their own behavior. This is especially true of celebrities, politicians, CEOs and athletes, according to Adam Galinsky, a behavioral psychologist at the Kellogg School of Management at Northwestern University in Evanston, Illinois. In a study with about 350 subjects, his team of researchers found that giving these kinds of people power makes them feel entitled and causes a disconnect in their judgment. It's "moral hypocrisy," says Galinsky. Put another way, it's the product of multiplying *ought times inward-bound.* It's why, 75 percent of the time, the problem is not the problem. Companies characterized as entitled are unlikely to enjoy long-term success at being truly innovative.

But it gets worse. When we add fear to narcissism, we get cultures characterized by victimhood.

Ought-Is-Can-Will

27

VICTIMHOOD
Human Energy = Is x Inward-Bound

> Self-pity is easily the most destructive of the nonpharmaceutical narcotics; it is addictive, gives momentary pleasure and separates the victim from reality.
>
> —*John W. Gardner*

Since 2004, Bill Cosby has been ranting against a culture of victimhood.

At the NAACP gala commemorating the 50th anniversary of *Brown v. Board of Education*, Bill Cosby's frustration boiled over. He believes African-American men are acting like victims looking to be coddled instead of taking responsibility. "Everybody knows how important it is to speak English except these knuckleheads. You can't land a plane with 'Why you ain't…'" Since 2004, "A Call Out with Bill Cosby" has been challenging the therapeutic culture and in various places has been well received. "People have been waiting to hear the truth, they don't want to be coddled," says Cosby.

When a large group of people multiply *is times inward-bound*, you get a culture of victimhood. Companies are not exempt from this phenomenon. Inward-bound leaders produce different cultures. A culture of entitlement thinks in terms of *ought*—people enculturated in this tradition believe they ought to be given preferential treatment. A culture of victimhood thinks in terms of *is*—people enculturated in this tradition believe they are victims of circumstances. They don't demand preferential treatment. They want protection. Thus, this is a dominant attitude of unions and union negotiations. Much of the auto industries woes over time can be seen as the clash of inflated (management) vs. victim (workers). In the meantime, the reality of Asian automakers marched right on by without giving them a sideward glance.

I've worked with a company that was hard hit by the recession of 2008. For the first time in their history, they had to lay off a fair number of workers. In exit interviews, the company's leaders were surprised at how many employees that were terminated imagined the company as a safe sanctuary. It was supposed to protect them. When they were laid off, some of them acted like victims.

This company is pretty serious about a moral DNA and culture. But somehow, some way, "culture" came to mean: "We will never lose our jobs. This is a safe place to work." To their credit, the CEO realizes they still have much work to do.

Sequencing E=cc indicates that many companies have cultures of victimhood. You see it most when tough get tough. Inward-bound institutions are out of touch with reality. When the leaders mostly pay attention to the present circumstances and "the way it is," the company's culture can easily begin to assume life is a series of circumstances largely beyond their control. The auto industry would qualify on this count. I grew up in Michigan. The Big Three created a culture that was very attractive to individuals who wanted a company to be their safe sanctuary. "Thirty And Out" was the mantra. But the introduction of higher quality Japanese cars to the American market as well as the oil crisis in 1973 caused the unions to assume the posture of a victim. They have since tried to take the auto industry emotionally hostage. "It's not our fault." "This is how we've always done it." Management of course isn't helpful. "All that and a bag of chips" exacerbated the antagonistic relationship between management and labor. It's unlikely the U.S. auto industry will be innovative in the long run if these two cultures continue to clash.

Companies with cultures of victimhood attract workers who have trouble seeing the big picture. They fail to appreciate how markets evolve, new markets emerge, and economies rise and fall. "We've always done it this way" can get slammed into the rocks of reality. I was recently talking to a retiree of a company that used to be headquartered close to where I live. He was lamenting the fact that the local plant once employed 3,000 workers in three shifts running 'round the clock. "Now the whole operation is in Mexico, and I can't understand why." He was talking like a victim. Companies that are the product of multiplying *is times inward-bound* create cultures of victimhood. When times hit, employees get sucked deeper into the vortex of victimhood. "What did *I* do wrong?"

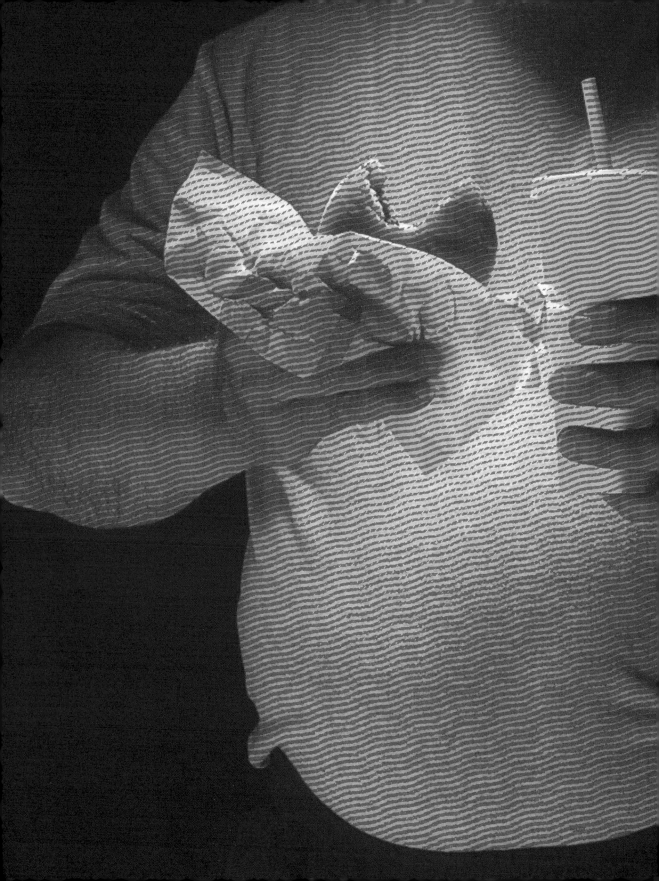

The fact is, this retiree probably did nothing wrong. His dilemma is more the result of an institutional culture that caused his particular company to sink rather than swim. From the top down, the C-level leaders postured that their company was an unfortunate victim of unfair trade practices. This veneer of victimhood does not serve people well when tough times hit. Union leaders for example can get so wrapped around the axle of saving jobs (theirs included) that they fail to see larger issues at play. Broadening their perspective would require a candid consensus of what the company culture looks like from leaders outside the organization. Most "victim" organizations only hear "atta boys" from admirers. Companies characterized by this culture slowly but surely feel threatened by anyone not enthusiastically espousing the party line.

This culture of victimhood however has larger ramifications than simply infecting much of Corporate America. The truth is, America is becoming a nation of victims. There are many critical issues that Americans can't talk about because the mere mention of them hurts someone's feelings. We're being taken hostage by a culture of victimhood.

For example, engineering firms report increasing difficulty designing airtight respirators to protect American factory workers and firefighters. The culprit? The changing shape of our faces. While 60% of Americans are overweight and 30% are obese, 87% of all firefighters, 73% of American healthcare workers and 91% of those in law enforcement are overweight or obese. But we can't talk about this.

Once upon a time humans got along fine on two daily meals. Improved agricultural production and food distribution bumped us to "three squares a day." By 1957, the average fast food hamburger contained 210 calories. Today it's 618. The average bag of movie theater popcorn had 170 calories 40 years ago. Today it's 900. Taco Bell now offers the "fourth meal" while the Mall of America in Minneapolis sells deep fried Twinkies and Snickers bars. We're full of it.

But *we're* not to blame. It's the candy companies.

The tightening belt affects health care and fuel consumption. *The Economist* reports that given the current rise of Type II diabetes, the American health care system will be overwhelmed in twenty years. Type II diabetes is usually preventable by exercise and proper diet. At the pump, each extra pound of body weight in all of today's vehicles results in the need for more than 39 million gallons of extra gasoline usage each year. In a recent issue of the journal *The Engineering Economist,* scientists calculated that the tab for overweight people in a vehicle—with gas prices averaging $3 a gallon—amounts to $7.7 million a day, or $2.8 billion a year. How are we going to begin to address these problems if we're all victims?

Jack Welch of General Electric did a good job of keeping GE from becoming inward-bound. He got involved in the details of selling things such as jet engines. He knew that taking responsibility for individual customer relationships—and making other senior executives do the same—is one of the best ways to discover what a company is doing right and what it should be doing differently. It keeps an organization from acting like a victim and taking responsibility for screw-ups.

But these kinds of company cultures are rare. More often than not, you see cultures as the product of multiplying *is times inward-bound*, where employees simply want a safe job. There is no real passion for the work. It's simply a job. But it's safe.

Or so we thought, until the recent economic crisis.

Two hundred years ago, Tocqueville warned of a "soft despotism" in which Americans would increasingly look to the state as a security blanket. "His analysis must be extended in our time," Matthew Crawford suggests: "The softly despotic tendencies of a nanny state are found in the large commercial enterprise as well, and indeed a case could be made that it is now outsized corporations, more than the government, that exercise this particularly enervating form of authority in our lives, through work."

The reality is that there is no such thing as a "safe" place, be it work, religious institution, or gated community. Multiplying *is times inward-bound* does not yield an accurate assessment of human nature or reality. It's a skewed perception of reality along with a false sense of security. It does not create cultures that can innovate. Ask yourself: Do you lead a company characterized by a culture of victimhood? Companies with this culture are unlikely to enjoy long-term success at being truly innovative.

Neither are companies that hype their culture.

28

HYPED

Human Energy = Can x Inward-Bound

> Don't believe the hype.
>
> —*Public Enemy*

Where'd all this talk about "passion" come from?

The New York Times columnist David Brooks asks how magazine editors—month after month, year after year—can churn out "page after page on lip-gloss trends, armoire placement, or powerboat design" without getting depressed. The answer? "These editors have to use their favorite word, *passion*."

When you multiply *ought times inward-bound*, you get entitlement. When you multiply *is times inward-bound*, you get victimhood. When you multiply *can times inward-bound,* you get a culture that's hyped. Workers enculturated in these traditions don't take seriously the ought-is-can-will code. When company leaders talk about "corporate culture," it's wink-wink, nod-nod. Few take it seriously since everyone knows we're not talking about reality. "Passion comes from reality," writes Dallas Willard.

When companies have cultures that workers perceive as wired into everyday reality— that is, the corporate culture shapes hiring, firing, bonuses, incentives, products, processes, and policies—passion is not a problem. It's not even an issue. Some things only become conspicuous by their absence. When you multiply *can times inward-bound*, the culture hypes "principles" and "values" and "passion"—which indicates that workers assume we're not talking about reality. Hence, there is no passion. These kinds of companies hire people to pump the passion. It's a culture of hype.

This is why passion has become one of our biggest buzzwords of the last 20 years. It has, in case you haven't noticed. I teach a course to postgraduate students every year. Near the beginning of the course, I ask them to collect every reference to passion that they can over the course of one week. There are generally 13 students in the class and they usually come back with more than 50 references to passion in everyday advertising. In 2008, for instance, Langham Auckland launched a winter weekend package called "Passionate for Prada." "Diabetes Is Our Passion," Novartis advertises. What makes George Washington University's MBA program great? Passion. Pierce Brosnan is pursuing his two great passions—environmentalism and movies. Bratz has a passion for fashion slippers and flip-flops. Yanni sells *Reflections of Passion.* Lauryn Hill's got "The Passion." The Cure is cuter—"Plastic Passion." Duran Duran—"Of Crime and Passion." Jimmy Buffett—"Cuban Crime of Passion." Stop the madness!

I find references to passion everywhere. Rosemary Augustine's *How to Live and Work Your Passion and Still Earn a Living* describes how to "maximize your potential for optimal career growth, journal your way to self-discovery and find your passion." At Starbucks, I saw a poster on the wall that read: "Ignite a fire the siren said and feel its power. It is fire that roasts our coffees and it is fire that forges a personality, lifting it out of the grey and coloring it with heat, passion, and intensity." I like Starbucks, but is this reality? In the fine phrase of Shakespeare, "The lady doth protest too much, methinks."

One of my profs in grad school used to remind his students: "If you have to go around announcing that you're the man of the house, someone obviously hasn't gotten the message." If a company has to go around and hype the culture, someone obviously isn't getting the message. Why does this happen? Do the multiplication math.

Leaders with an inward-bound conscience generally don't see the big picture—ought-is-can-will. Their focus is *inward*, on themselves and the company. Being can-do people, they only think in terms of *can*. But reality is bigger than *can*—it's *ought* and *is* and *will*. Thus, when these kinds of leaders shape company culture, workers perceive that we're not talking enough about reality. Passion comes from reality.

Married couples tend to talk more about passion when there is a lack of passion in their marriage. They talk more about their sex life when there is a conspicuous absence of sex. If on the other hand a marriage is firing on all cylinders, the couple doesn't spend much time chattering about it. Passion comes from reality.

That's why there has been a conspicuous rise recently in the chatter over "passion"—and some marked skepticism. In reality, it indicates that many corporate cultures are disconnected from reality. When business guru Richard Florida for example claims that Best Buy's work environment is designed to "unleash the power of all of our people as they have fun while being the best," some observers see it as merely hype. "Where I live, Best Buy seems to be starting people at $8.00 an hour," writes MIT economist Frank Levy. He doesn't buy the hype. It sounds dangerously close to fanaticism.

The philosopher George Santayana said, "Fanaticism consists in redoubling your effort when you have forgotten your aim." When can-do leaders fail to take into account the entire code, they create cultures of hype—the product of *can times inward-bound*. What compounds the problem is that these same insulated leaders often delegate the work of making culture to hired guns. This exacerbates the need for more exaggeration, since workers notice that company leaders are conspicuous by their absence. When creating a company culture becomes a matter of hired guns, professionally produced videos, and clever catch phrases, you've got a hyped culture. No one will be particularly passionate about it, since everyone knows we're not talking about reality. This kind of culture is characteristic of Corporate America but not limited to it.

In her essay "A Vindication of Love," Cristina Nehring suggests that our modern, run-and-gun culture has drained relationships of excitement and purged them of Eros. Result? A great deal of literature about "passion" because of so many passionless marriages. Don't believe the hype. In 2009, Sandra Tsing Loh autopsied her own failed marriage along with those of her peers. High achievers all, she suggested the quest for security and success turned them into sexless drudges. Culture carries the day.

These essayists are bright and witty. They've graduated from some of our best schools. They've made it a point to live in and around the cultural creatives and participate in the arts and local get-togethers. So where's the passion? It's gone because they intuitively sense that their work and their aims are not well connected to reality. The result is people and organizations hyping passion. But that's not the problem. Less reality, less passion. We need cultures that are better connected to reality.

If your company is operating with an accurate assessment of reality, passion has some positives. In the positive sense, passion comes from the idea of strong emotion, desire, suffering, or enduring. Human beings operate by *desire*. People endure what they perceive as *real*. If a company sequences E=cc and has the right culture, they can promote proper passion. And they can drop the hype.

If however your company is *not* operating with an accurate assessment of reality, passion is a problem. It can easily blur our perception of reality. Companies with pragmatic leaders—that pretty much sums up most of Corporate America—need people who can see patterns, not just hype culture and leave the hard work of making it to consultants.

Companies characterized by hype are unlikely to enjoy long-term success at being truly innovative. They often miss "the way it ought to be" since that requires pulling the lens out and seeing the bigger picture. Because their culture is the result of multiplying *can times inward-bound*, workers sense a disconnect between walk and talk. Hence, it's all hype.

29

UTOPIAN

Human Energy = Will x Inward-Bound

> Futurism is the major mental disease of our time.
>
> —*George Orwell*

A lot of corporate leaders create "nowhere" cultures.

When company leaders have an *inward-bound conscience*, they create four kinds of cultures. *Inward-bound times ought* creates a culture of entitlement. Companies with a culture of victimhood are the product of *inward-bound times is*. *Inward-bound times can* creates a culture of hype. What is the culture that's the result of multiplying *inward-bound times will?* Organizations with *inward-bound* leaders who prefer *will* create cultures that spend a lot of time "casting vision" and rejiggering plans in the hopes of finding the grand program or the killer innovation. This culture is utopian. Workers encultured in this culture don't take seriously the ought-is-can-will code. When these *inward-bound* company leaders talk about "corporate culture," it too is wink-wink, nod-nod.

John Lennon and Paul McCartney wrote "Nowhere Man" in 1965. It's about a utopian man. *Utopia* literally means "nowhere," from the Greek *ou* "not" and *topos* "place." Thomas More used it as title of his book in 1516 about an imaginary island enjoying perfect legal, social, and political systems. But that's not reality. Utopian is "having no known location" in the sense of something being "impossibly visionary."

This is a uniquely American condition. David Brooks, in his 2004 book *On Paradise Drive*, writes that Americans today live (yet have always lived) in the future tense. This notion goes all the way back to the nation's founding. Whether it was "a city set on a hill" or Manifest Destiny, Americans have always preferred to live in the future.

If you operate with an accurate assessment of human nature, looking into the future is not a problem. But when it is disconnected from reality, you get pipe dreams. Success is always "just around the corner," or "this new program will make work far better," or "this event will change your life forever," or this new killer app will produce a "paradigm shift." It's utopian; the result of multiplying *will times inward-bound*.

Utopian leaders don't understand that it takes time, typically ten years, for a corporate culture to gain traction and make a difference on the shop floor or in sales or in products. Utopian cultures don't have that kind of patience and stamina. Inward-bound leaders do not demonstrate a capacity to think on a larger scale (i.e., the code) and longer term (i.e., how hard it is to properly sequence E=cc). These companies cannot be innovative over the long haul; they never become great.

Jim Collins writes that great companies understand that those "who launch revolutions, dramatic change programs, and wrenching restructurings... never happened in one fell swoop. There was no defining action, no grand program, no one killer innovation, no solitary lucky break, no miracle moment." Companies characterized by utopian cultures don't get this. Their leaders are too detached from everyday reality to understand how arduous it is to change a culture. It's more like turning around an aircraft carrier than a dinghy. Inward-bound leaders don't understand this. Making a healthy culture is, as Collins writes, a process resembling "relentlessly pushing a giant flywheel in one direction, turn upon turn, building momentum until it reaches a point of breakthrough, and beyond."

I had firsthand experience in this fresh out of college. I worked for an organization that mentored college students. Surprisingly, within a few years, I was promoted to rank of director and was thereby invited to regional meetings. It was at these meetings that I gained a bigger picture of how the organization was doing. It was not good. The numbers were down—fewer students were involved in our organization.

The higher ups, our supervisors from Corporate, kept coming up with plans and programs to gin up the numbers. One included a ridiculously expensive program driven entirely by PowerPoint. That went over like a lead balloon. It was a pipe dream of a program created by utopian leaders. We were in free-fall and no one knew what to do.

Over time I discovered why my particular campus was an anomaly (our numbers were up and everyone else's were down). It didn't take an Einstein. It turned out that most of the campus directors had, over time, lost touch with students. I learned that the average director was on campus to meet with students, on average, 1.5 hours *a week*. We were being paid to work 40 hours a week and expected to be meeting with students for most of that time. We had become an inward-bound organization.

Upon closer examination, it turned out that conscience was playing a role in shaping the organization's culture. One summer I worked in personnel and learned of a dramatic rise in new staff coming from broken homes, tough family backgrounds, or past drug abuse that made these new hires somewhat insecure or inward-bound. When they became directors, they looked for "easy" students who wouldn't challenge their leadership. Those students were hard to find. Hence, directors had 38.5 hours a week of free time. That was plenty of time to "imagine the possibilities" and gin up utopian plans.

Our annual conferences became theaters of the absurd—real nowhere plans. When we saw sparse results, utopia became more about "communication techniques" and crafting better "plans" and imagining a "preferred future" that would garner better results. It was futurism based on fantasy.

"Futurism is the major mental disease of our time," George Orwell wrote. Cultural analyst Os Guinness adds fuel to the futurism fire. He writes that it's "a quack science, it picks up current trends, projects them into the future, and then pretends that results are predictions." Utopian cultures quack because they don't understand human nature. They fail to appreciate how long it takes to change a culture. They want the quick-and-easy program, a one-size-fits-all approach. To sell the latest and greatest program, they forecast what the weather will be like in a few months.

The reality is that weather forecasting is a very inexact science. Four days out, forecasts are generally only 20 percent accurate. I've once worked with a company that had a 70 percent turnover rate because the company leadership was inward-bound. When they forecasted what the company culture was going to look like in the future, eyes rolled. When the culture didn't change, they blamed the workers. I never saw the personnel director assume any responsibility. He hired, and workers had one week to perform or else. He would often recall how *he* was able to perform these tasks years ago, so *anyone* should be able to. I later found out that he had not been on the shop floor for years. He had lost touch with the reality of what actually happened in the company's cubicles.

When you see organizations continually planning and reorganizing and implementing programs and re-implementing newer programs, you're looking at a company with a culture that's out-of-touch with reality. It's the result of engineering-types who are the corporate leaders, preferring *will* yet being *inward-bound.* They gin up plans based on an inaccurate assessment of human nature. They cannot be innovative for the long-term.

These first eight cultures, created by inflated or inward-bound leaders, cannot innovate over the long haul. What kinds of cultures are characterized by the third row in the matrix? What happens when you sequence *ought-is-can-will* through a shattered conscience?

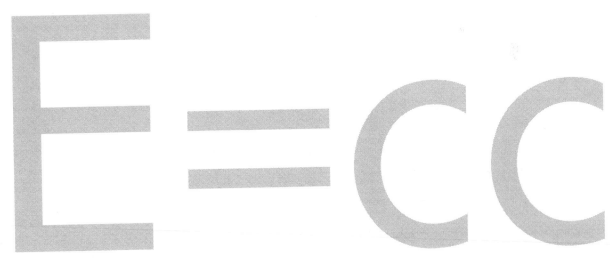

30

IDEAS BEFORE PEOPLE
Human Energy = Ought x Shattered

> It was the usual tale of intellectual idealism. Ideas before people, Mankind with a capital M, before men and women, wives, sons, or daughters.
>
> —*Paul Johnson*

Big ideas sure have made many people feel small.

Historian Paul Johnson's fascinating investigation into the lives of intellectual leaders reveals a troubling trait. In *The Intellectuals,* which traces the lives of various luminaries, Johnson found arrogance but also a disturbing indifference to people. This is what happens when the arrogant conscience bends too far and shatters. Gifted individuals and institutions that believe they know best for others place *ideas before people.* It's what happens when you multiply *ought times shattered.*

Ernest Hemingway emerges as an arrogant writer who worked hard at developing his style. Yet he did it at the expense of any concern for the women who loved him. Multiplying *ought times shattered* yields towering individuals who shape the institutions that often believe they hold the keys to a collective wisdom that is good for all. Johnson cites such figures as Jean-Jacques Rousseau, Percy Bysshe Shelley, Karl Marx, Leo Tolstoy, Jean-Paul Sartre, Bertrand Russell, Lillian Hellman, and others—with a final chapter commenting more briefly on figures such as George Orwell, Norman Mailer, and Noam Chomsky. All of them, at various times in their lives, exhibited an indifference to people. It was ideas before people.

"Beware of intellectuals," Johnson concludes. "Not only should they be kept well away from the levers of power, they should also be objects of particular suspicion

when they seek to offer collective advice." Why should we beware of these individuals and institutions? This way of seeing the world—through a lens rendering people and organizations almost completely unaware of self and others—might account for such dehumanizing practices as modern management.

Frederick Winslow Taylor is the father of modern management theory. Born in 1856 to a stern Quaker mother, young Frederick was a brilliant and determined lad. He believed sports ought to be played more efficiently. So he tinkered with new groundstrokes in tennis. He developed new types of clubs, fairway grasses, and soil mixtures in golf. It paid off. Taylor was the 1881 national doubles tennis champion and the handicap champion at the Philadelphia Country Club in 1902, 1903, and 1905. But it also *didn't* pay off.

Taylor put ideas before people. Sports were nothing more than mastery. He "was so obsessed with refining the rules and techniques of the many sports he played that he reportedly took all the fun out of the neighborhood games as a child," Maggie Jackson writes in *Distracted: The Erosion of Attention and the Coming Dark Age*. When Taylor turned to the workaday world in the late 1870s, his ideas on how work ought to be done yielded the science of industrial psychology, human resources, performance evaluation, quality control, and management studies. He would eventually come to have as much influence on the world as that of Marx or Freud, according to management guru Peter Drucker. Even Lenin was a convert. "We should try every scientific and progressive suggestion of the Taylor system." Marxists did try them—and just look at all the fun they had.

The problem is Taylor's management ideas don't fit human nature. In 1899, the Bethlehem Steel Company asked Taylor to improve worker efficiency. He started with a simple question: How many tons of pig-iron bars can a worker load onto a railcar in the course of a working day? Taylor reviewed company records, estimated the rate at which the laborers loaded iron, and offered to double the workers' wages if they worked harder. It killed them.

Taylor's solution was firing the workers and hiring "high-priced men"—Pennsylvania Dutchman—whose intelligence he compared to that of an ox. That's right—animals. They came close to meeting the goals and Taylor went on to write *The Principles of*

Scientific Management. When Bethlehem Steel's profits didn't increase, they fired Taylor, throwing out his systems. But Taylor continued to defend his ideas.

Taylor's ideas might have died then had he not woven the theories in *Scientific Management* into an overlapping network of leading culture-shaping institutions of the day. In the spring of 1908, Taylor met with Harvard professors and later that year Harvard opened the first graduate school in the country to offer a master's degree in business. It was based on one assumption: people ought to be "managed" by "experts." It was an idea that came before people. It was not based on an accurate assessment of human nature. The first assembly line workers recognized this.

In his engaging book *Shop Class as Soulcraft: An Inquiry Into the Value of Work*, Matthew Crawford recounts how Ford workers simply walked out when Henry Ford introduced the assembly line in 1913. It was too dehumanizing. "The new system provoked natural revulsion," Crawford writes. It also seemed to produce natural selection—downward. At the close of 1913, Ford estimated they'd have to replenish the factory ranks with 100 workers. It was necessary to hire 963. Change, however, is usually most evident in the beginning. Slowly but surely, workers became habituated to this de-evolutionary process. That's the subtle power of culture. Today, most assembly line workers think little about the drone-like drabness of their daily work. Some *feel* it—and trudge through their toils in the hope of "thirty and out." It's why economics was referred to in the nineteenth century as the "dismal science," because of the dreary nature of factory work. But it's not the way it ought to be.

"Taylor destroyed the romance of work," writes Drucker. "Instead of a noble 'skill', [work became] a series of simple notions." A behavioral DNA codes people. It makes us yearn for a sense of "work signature"—that our work matters and we have a hand in making it. Managing people often destroys that. Multiplying *ought times shattered* yields individuals and institutions where ideas, such as managing people, come before people. That's not innovation. Before Taylor's time, it was assumed that individuals and institutions only manage animals, appetites, and assets. The idea that we "manage people" replaced the earlier notion that leaders *mentor* people. Mentoring is a less efficient but more effective way of shaping the conscience of colleagues. It requires a great deal of time spent with protégés, generally starts with a simple "follow me," and always includes the experiential "I'll show you and then you try it." It was once viewed as the most effective way to create self-aware people.

Is modern management the result of a lens lacking self-awareness? We can't properly sequence E=cc if we don't first accurately define reality. Is your company characterized by *ought times shattered?* Companies that put ideas before people are unlikely to enjoy long-term success at being truly innovative.

31

POWER BEFORE PEOPLE
Human Energy = Is x Shattered

Let whatever is smoldering erupt . . .

—From the writing of three journalists who incited the Hutus to massacre the
Tutsis

"It is what it is" can get ugly.

The twentieth century has demonstrated that major wars are not necessary for
individuals and institutions to wreak havoc. Between 1900 and 1987 almost 170 million
people were murdered by governments—far more than the 34.4 million killed in wars.
Hitler, Stalin, and Mao account for more than 100 million of those murdered. Pol Pot—
in just four years—killed about a third of Cambodia's population. It's power before
people. It's might makes right.

Under Saddam Hussein, at least 290,000 Iraqis disappeared. These grim statistics
are part of a twentieth-century atrocity called "democide," a term coined by Dr. R.
J. Rummel, a professor of political science at the University of Hawaii. Democide
describes government's intentional killing because of ideas—not war. Does *is times
shattered* account for the twentieth century's democides, genocides, and homicides?

Democide includes government-sponsored killings for political reasons. It's
intentionally or knowingly exhibiting a reckless and depraved disregard for life, such as
forced mass starvation. Democide includes incarcerating people in camps where they
soon die of malnutrition, unattended disease, and forced labor. It's deporting them into
wastelands where they may die rapidly from exposure and disease. It's power before
people. It's the Golden Rule: He who has the gold, rules.

Only individuals and institutions with the power to exterminate large numbers of people can perform democide. The ruthlessness is rooted in a lack of self-awareness. It is cruel because these individuals and the institutions they rule disdain any sort of moral code—except that *might makes right*. Where did that idea originate?

It was referred to in 1846 by the abolitionist Adin Ballou. He, as was the case with Abraham Lincoln, embraced the reverse: *right makes might*. That idea was rooted in a moral code. We hear it in Lincoln's landmark abolitionist speech at Cooper Union in 1860: "Let us have faith that right makes might, and in that faith, let us, to the end, dare to do our duty as we understand it." Not everyone agreed.

Five years later, on the morning of April 14, 1865, John Wilkes Booth learned that Lincoln would be attending a play that evening in Washington. He wrote a note to his mother, justifying the murder since "might makes right." Yes, those were his very words. At 10:00 p.m., Booth slipped into the presidential box at Ford's Theatre and fatally shot Lincoln.

Multiplying *is times shattered* yields individuals and institutions that have an unflinching attitude toward the present reality. In the case of artists who shrug "It is what it is," the impact is minimal. Whatever. But in the case of those who create cultures of "whatever," they promote or permit democide, genocide, and homicide. Hellacious.

We saw it in the story that came out of Africa in 2003. Nine years after the genocide in Rwanda, the International Criminal Tribunal judged that the three journalists who incited the Hutus to massacre the Tutsis, writing words such as "Let whatever is smoldering erupt," were guilty because they were responsible for the words they wrote. With freedom of expression came responsibility, the court argued.

The blood of 800,000 Rwandans cries out against "whatever." Multiplying *is times shattered* yields individuals and institutions that put power before people. Perhaps the most powerful example is the prevalence of triangulation in companies.

Triangulation is talking behind the back of colleagues. It's when an individual "confides" to another or simply "unloads their soul," or "processes" with one colleague about another, when that other colleague is not present. Couched as confidential, the net effect

is a negative impression of the person being discussed. It's not only wrong; it's deadly. It makes a mockery of integrity and obedience to the unenforceable because integrity is not only what you say but *to whom* you say it. Triangulation is taking out a colleague with sniper fire. It's character assassination. It's using power to assassinate another's reputation. The problem is compounded because snipers leave no trace of their presence. No cartridge shells left lying around. A friend of mine was recently slandered in the company that he just left—but no one can source who took the shot. "It is what it is" is all they can say. Whatever. My friend was glad to leave a culture of *is times shattered*, but he cannot restore his reputation with some former colleagues.

This incident is an example of the power of culture. People probably weren't *consciously* thinking: "Let's ruin a reputation!" Instead, we act more on impulse or intuition, as enculturated beings. A corporate culture formed by an inflated conscience will be cocky. A corporate culture formed by an inward-bound conscience will emphasize compliance.

A corporate culture formed by a shattered conscience will be indifferent—or worse. It can also produce catastrophic horrors. That's why "whatever" is the result of multiplying *is times shattered*. "Whatever" couldn't care less about character assassination or triangulation or democide or murder. It questions whether truth counts anymore.

This kind of culture might explain the alarming increase in horrific crimes. In the summer of 2008, Scott Johnson murdered three teenagers in northern Michigan. In a *New Yorker* piece, Calvin Trillin tells the terrible tale of Johnson who had always been a drifter— through the army, marriage, and assorted dead-end jobs. Johnson ended up believing other people were the source of his problems. Feeling powerless to improve his lot in life, Johnson turned to power—in this case, a high-powered rifle. He went "off the grid," fled to the Upper Peninsula of Michigan where his mother lived and began to stash a cache of weapons and gear near a railroad crossing high over the Menominee River. One summer day, Tiffany Pohlson, Anthony Spigarelli, Katrina Coates, and Derek Barnes swam across the river and headed for a rock to do some diving. When the group was 15 to 20 feet away, Johnson jumped from his hiding place, opened fire, and killed Pohlson and Spigarelli. He then turned and continued shooting at some people swimming in the river, killing Bryan Mort.

When Johnson was later convicted of murder, he read a prepared speech at the close of the trial. Trillin writes of the lesson that Johnson said he learned at the age of twelve: "The truth of the matter at hand is that the truth doesn't count anymore. It is the quality of the lie that endures." Where did he get the idea that "the truth doesn't matter anymore"?

Does a world where the truth doesn't matter anymore place power before people? We can't properly sequence E=cc if we don't first accurately define reality. How many of today's organizations' cultures are characterized by *is times shattered*? Companies characterized as "power before people" are unlikely to enjoy long-term success at being truly innovative.

32

VALUELESS VALUES
Human Energy = Can x Shattered

> "We never do evil so fully and cheerfully as when we do it out of conscience.
>
> —*Blaise Pascal*

Does your company promote a set of "core values"?

When company leaders have a shattered conscience, they create four kinds of cultures. *Shattered times ought* creates a culture of *ideas over people.* Companies with a culture of *power over people* are the product of *shattered times is. Shattered times can* creates a culture of "valueless values." When these shattered company leaders talk about "corporate culture" and values, workers treat it like wink-wink, nod-nod. If you don't believe me, ask yourself: does your company have a "values statement?"

Most organizations have developed a set of "core values." But they might be *valueless.* Especially if they are the product of multiplying *can times* a *shattered* conscience—what amounts to an unprincipled pragmatism. It's certainly not innovation. In this case, most companies are blithely unaware that today's values are essentially valueless. It has to do with the origin of the idea of values. Even Margaret Thatcher didn't know where values first popped up.

During her election campaign in 1983, Thatcher said that she was grateful to have been brought up by a Victorian grandmother who taught her those values: hard work, self-reliance, self-respect, cleanliness, neighborliness, and pride in country. "All of these things," she said, "are Victorian values. They are also perennial values."

Not quite. What Thatcher couldn't see was that her grandmother would not have spoken of them as "values." She would have spoken of them as "virtues." Historian Gertrude

Himmelfarb observes that prior to the nineteenth century, business used the language of virtues. Virtues are vertical, rooted in a code: (1) how things ought to be; (2) what is—i.e., what things look like in the workaday world; (3) what we can do to make things better, to fix or repair things; and (4) what things will be like some day. Virtues are rooted in the timeless and transcendent—they apply to everyone everywhere all the time, even in business.

Values, on the other hand, are horizontal and merely preferences. The German philosopher Friedrich Nietzsche noted that the removal of all moral codes, such as ought-is-can-will, meant life no longer had any transcendent meaning. Nietzsche said moral ideas are now entirely subjective, mere customs and conventions—they are values. "Values, as we now understand them, can be whatever any individual, group, or society chooses for any reason," Himmelfarb notes. "This impartial, 'non-judgmental' sense of values is now so firmly entrenched in our vocabulary that one can hardly imagine a time without it."

Nietzsche understood that values have nothing to do with human conscience. He agreed that conscience is the cardinal distinction between man and animal, but like Darwin, he dismissed the critical role of conscience in governing human and institutional behavior. Nietzsche predicted that the twentieth century would be a century of "wars such as have never happened on earth," wars catastrophic beyond all imagining. Why? "If the doctrines . . . of the lack of any cardinal distinction between man and animal," he wrote, "are hurled into the people for another generation . . . then nobody should be surprised when . . . brotherhoods with the aim of the robbery and exploitation of the non-brothers . . . will appear in the arena of the future."

Nietzsche went on to warn of a period more dreadful than the great wars, a time of "the total eclipse of all values" in a frantic period of "revaluation," in which people would try to find new systems of values to replace the old moral codes.

We witness the futility of trying to make values valuable in today's business world. According to a recent *Harvard Business Review* article, business people usually don't act on their values while at work. Researchers Judith Samuelson and Mary Gentile write that workers instead view ethics training and values statements as "time-outs," pulling them away from "real" work. "They talked about being derailed by these issues, not because they felt morally ambivalent but because dealing with these issues is simply not what they do." Why do they make this assumption?

They learn it from the prevailing culture. Cultures are composed of overlapping networks of ideas, images, individuals, institutions, and the items they produce. Since the 1960s, college students have been told no one's values are better than anyone else's. This new relativism denies there are things that are intrinsically high and others that are intrinsically low. Instead, today's values are squishy, like Jell-O. But products, personnel, and profit-and-loss statements—they're solid, like trees. As anyone knows, you can't nail Jell-O to a tree. Institutions end up with valueless values.

What's the solution?

Samuelson and Gentile suggest the answer to ethical lapses lies in broadening the scope of what colleagues understand to be a part of "real" work. "Managers who view their professional purpose in broad terms have an easier time with ethical questions." Broadening the story line would include *ought* as Chapter One. That would require properly sequencing an organization's DNA, using E=cc. *That* would be innovative.

Modern management theory is infected with this fact/value divide. Facts are the "hard" stuff of the company—profits and products. They *matter*. Values are the "soft" stuff—people and ethics. This confusion leads companies to apply technological solutions—training videos and ethics seminars—to moral and political problems. This is an inaccurate assessment of human nature and reality. The unreality of this dichotomy might be becoming apparent to some. In 1995, *The Washington Post* featured op-ed articles on the need for a new moral center and another deploring the medicalization of teenage pregnancy. The columnist said teenage pregnancy is a moral, not a medical problem. At the same time, the cover of *Newsweek* was emblazoned with the word "Shame" and below it the subtitle, "How Do We Bring Back a Sense of Right and Wrong?" Great question. Multiplying *can times a shattered* conscience certainly isn't the answer.

Companies that constantly pump up "values" are tipping their hand. They don't have an accurate assessment of human nature. Thus, they don't understand conscience, which is critical to the long-term success of truly innovative companies.

33

PRACTICALITY BEFORE PEOPLE
Human Energy = Will x Shattered

> Most ordinary Americans don't think about the power of ideas. We're practical. But with that often comes an inability to understand the ideas that impel people.
>
> — *James Billington*

Blithely unaware companies don't appear to be a problem—they're "practical."

Company leaders with shattered consciences create four different kinds of cultures. Multiplying *ought times shattered* creates a culture of *ideas over people*. Multiplying *is times shattered* produces a culture of *power* over *people*. Multiplying *can times shattered* creates a culture of *valueless values*. And then finally, furthest to the right in the matrix, multiplying *will times a shattered conscience* creates a culture where company leaders primarily think *practicality* over *people*. If this thing called "culture" *works*, they're all for it. What's wrong with that?

The problem with this kind of practicality is that it's reductionism. Several years after launching AES, Dennis Bakke and Roger Sant had a group of leaders of the company together to discuss how things had gone with regard to creating the company culture. A couple of the vice presidents had been skeptical early on in the process, Bakke reports. Now their attitudes had changed. They thought the culture was "fantastic." They went on: "We love these values. They really work." Bakke writes: "There was dead silence, and both Roger and I turned somewhat white and thought to ourselves, we have, in fact, done something very wrong. We didn't choose these values because we thought they would work. We chose these values because they are right."

Multiplying *will times a shattered conscience* creates a culture where company leaders have no peripheral vision. Culture translates into functionality, efficiency, and profitability. It is wise to remember that torture is the most "practical" way to get people to talk. But that doesn't make it right. Bakke understands that companies fixated on functionality and practicality treat culture like wink-wink, nod-nod. But that's not all there is to this story.

The second problem with practical people is that they don't appreciate how ideas and images and institutions—cultures—shape people. They don't understand human nature. Leaders who only value "what works" fail to see how overlapping networks of institutions shape culture, and how culture indirectly but most effectively shapes our desires that shape our behavior. They instead assume everyone bobs above culture— that you can balance atop a beach ball while floating in the ocean waves. They discount culture because of their assumption that we make choices independent of culture. That's what Andy Sachs assumed about her choices in clothing—until Miranda Priestly dressed her down.

Andy Sachs was the young assistant to Miranda Priestley in *The Devil Wears Prada.* Skeptical that Paris fashion trends and the fashion industry shape her wardrobe choices, Andy scoffs at the fancy belts that "all look the same to me." This elitist culture that convulses over belt colors has nothing to do with her choices. At least that's what Andy assumes to be true... until she is caught scoffing. Her boss, Miranda, overhears the scoff.

Miranda wheels around to Andy who backpedals by saying she's "still learning about this *stuff.*" Oops. "This . . . *stuff?*" asks Miranda. "*Stuff?*"

> Oh . . . Okay. You think this "stuff" has nothing to do with you. You . . . go to your closet and select—I don't know—that lumpy blue sweater for instance because you're trying to tell the world that you take yourself too seriously to care about what you put on your back. But what you don't know is that sweater is not just blue, it's not turquoise . . . it's not lapis . . . it's actually cerulean. And you're also blithely unaware of the fact that in 2002 Oscar de la Renta did a collection of cerulean gowns.

And then I think it was Yves Saint Laurent who showed cerulean military gowns . . . and then cerulean quickly showed up in the collections of eight different designers. And then it filtered down through the department stores . . . and then trickled on down to some tragic Casual Corner where you no doubt fished it out of some clearance bin. However, that blue represents millions of dollars and countless jobs . . . and it's sort of comical how you think that you've made a choice that exempts you from the fashion industry when, in fact, you're wearing a sweater that was selected for you by the people in this room.

From a pile of . . . *stuff*.

"Practical" leaders sniff at culture as simply being *a pile of stuff*. For their companies, the bottom line is: "Does this work?" These leaders create companies that are blithely unaware of how ideas such as "passion" and "values" (or cultures of presumptuousness, or being cocksure, or feeling entitled) quickly show up in workers' attitudes and actions. These "practical" leaders comically assume that workers can *think* their way to better behavior—that obedience to the unenforceable is simply a matter of being trained to parrot principles of excellence. Their dismissal of culture is a uniquely American trait.

James Billington, librarian of Congress, chides Americans for their aversion to recognizing the power of ideas and culture. He writes: "Most ordinary Americans don't think about the power of ideas. We're practical. But with that often comes an inability to understand the ideas that impel people of different political cultures." Or, as John Maynard Keynes observed, "Practical men, who believe themselves to be quite exempt from any intellectual influences, are usually the slaves of some defunct economist. Madmen in authority, who hear voices in the air, are distilling their frenzy from some academic scribbler of a few years back . . . I am sure that the power of vested interests is vastly exaggerated compared with the gradual encroachment of ideas."

A third problem with practicality over people is that an overarching concern for practicality can rob workers of a sense of transcendence, reducing tasks to toil. Clear-eyed leadership reminds workers of the importance of the purpose and mission. They tirelessly elevate it to the level of transcendence. "Do you realize that what you're doing here matters?" A great leader lifts spirits until his or her arms ache. A naively pragmatic leader focuses only on practicality.

This is why, practically speaking, creating a corporate culture is not primarily conducting "corporate culture" training days. It is more a day-to-day process of connecting the culture to specific tasks. It is also helping colleagues *unlearn* the myth that culture is "what works." Doing the right thing does not always translate into higher profits and happier people. People who have seen culture used in companies merely for it's utilitarian value are rightly skeptical of the process but have to unlearn their skepticism. People come into an organization with a frame for reality and a set of assumptions. A friend of mine who runs a large company says most new hires are cynical of all this "culture" stuff because it's been reduced to "it's gotta be practical." Everyone brings a definition of reality into work. Unlearning doesn't happen overnight.

Finally, "practical" leaders show little patience for how long it takes to create a culture. They are tone deaf on how *worldviews* or frames of reference become *ways of life* and the way people perceive reality. Their bottom line is practicality. The problem with people devoted to practicality is that they usually apply technological solutions to problems that are, at bottom, moral, sociological, and philosophical . This leads companies to "neglect the social, moral, and political infrastructure on which our well-being depends," Matthew Stewart writes. *Infrastructure* is a twenty-dollar word for a company's *culture*.

This doesn't mean that companies should be impractical. "Practical vigor is a virtue," historian Richard Hofstadter writes. "What is spiritually crippling in our history is the tendency to make a mystique of practicality." Multiplying *will times shattered* yields companies that care about the code, conscience, and E=cc only if it's "practical." The irony is that they have practically no chance of enjoying long-term success at being truly innovative. They don't understand human conscience, the critical element.

So where are we in the matrix?

We've unpacked 12 of the 16 kinds of corporate conscience. Individuals and companies with inflated consciences dismiss their critics. Organizations with inward-bound consciences find their critics too disturbing or disruptive. This is why, after Jim Collins and his team of researchers had sorted through a list of 1,435 companies looking for those who enjoyed long-term innovation, they could only settle on 11 (my figure of

75 percent of companies being incapable of long-term innovation might be too low!). Inward-bound organizations only embrace in-house critiques, which are invariably weak. Individuals and companies with shattered consciences basically ignore their critics.

In all three cases—the inflated, inward-bound, and shattered consciences—company leaders create cultures that cannot innovate over the long haul since they cannot confront the brutal reality of their present circumstances. All innovation requires destruction.

The irony is that, in all three cases, these companies should appreciate that their *actions* point to a code. The problem is not behavior or the code. It's that their *attitudes* point them away from reality. The inflated culture treats a moral DNA as a formula for success. The inward-bound culture treats the code as fate—they can't do much about it. The shattered culture treats our human, moral DNA as a fiction.

It doesn't take a math whiz to see that these 12 cultures have an inaccurate assessment of human nature. They don't define reality very well. They are unlikely to enjoy long-term success at being truly innovative. To do that would require multiplying *clear-eyed conscience times the code*.

In the next four chapters, you'll see the kinds of companies that have an accurate assessment of human nature. They promote a clear-eyed conscience. They have what is critical to the long-term success of truly innovative companies.

They have *Camelot*.

34

WISE SAGE
Human Energy = Ought x Clear-eyed

> It ain't what you don't know that gets you into trouble. It's what you know for sure that just ain't so.
>
> —*Mark Twain*

Does your company have mentors or moralists?

When you multiply *ought times clear-eyed*, you get sages—men and women with graying hair and probing insights into human nature. They know the code and are clear-eyed about how business ought to be. A sage pulls the lens out and points out larger patterns at play—patterns that are often imperceptible to busy and pragmatic leaders. Wise sages can serve as mentors to these leaders. Wise organizations include them in their leadership circle.

In King Arthur's Roundtable, the wise sage was Merlin. When Merlin was absent from the roundtable—or if he was discounted—the kingdom was vulnerable. When organizations do not respect and institutionalize wise elders, they are vulnerable. One way to tell whether Merlin has a place at the table is to watch if eyes roll when a sage suggests that larger issues might be at play in a company's culture. A Merlin will pull the lens out, ask better questions, and often point out the possibility of unintended consequences. "It ain't what you don't know that gets you into trouble," Mark Twain observed. "It's what you know for sure that just ain't so." A Merlin questions the lens through which leaders see reality.

The reality today however is that most firms view mentors as impractical. C-level leaders see Merlin as interesting but inessential. Or companies confuse mentors with moralists.

I was recently talking with a corporate leader who assured me his organization had a Merlin. I know the company well and was dubious. So I asked for the mentor's name. My friend conceded that this man didn't understand the ought-is-can-will code. I suggested that individuals who don't know the code aren't mentors but moralists. They postulate pious platitudes about human behavior that don't hold water. Moralists understand souls but not systems. They are like team chaplains, helpful to individual athletes but incapable of changing the outcome of the game.

Merlins on the other hand are more like Alfie Kohn, whose research on financial incentives was mentioned in chapter 22. If companies embraced a sage such as Kohn, they'd consider carefully whether tangible rewards can actually lower levels of performance. "Study after study has shown that intrinsic interest in a task—the sense that something is worth doing for its own sake—typically declines when someone is given an external reason for doing it," Kohn writes. Findings from research indicate financial incentives actually undercut workers' motivation to take the organization's purpose seriously. Workers come to see themselves as working for money. Remember Jack Welch's defining moment that determines whether an organization takes its purpose seriously? It's when a colleague *doesn't* embrace the purpose but *is* hitting the numbers. Incentives can create this kind of culture. Unfortunately, most C-level leaders don't recognize this. That's because most organizations lack wise sages like Alfie Kohn.

Kohn notes there is not a single controlled study that "has shown a long-term improvement in the quality of work as a result of any reward system." In fact, scores of studies conducted in real workplaces have demonstrated how rewards tend to be powerfully counterproductive. When a manufacturing firm took Kohn's idea seriously, the incentive system that had been in place for its welders for years was removed. It was expected that production would slump with the incentives off the table, since it is assumed that financial incentives motivate people. This did happen at first. But then the welders' production rose and eventually reached a level as high as or higher than before. Why?

The secret is that workers need a sense of autonomy and higher purpose in their work. In a study conducted by Edward Deci, 90 participants were told to press a computer key every time a dot appeared on the screen. The researchers admitted it was a boring task but told the first group that it would be useful for other people learning about concentration. A second group was told the task "will be for your own good." The third group was only given instructions without explanation. The first group did the task better than the other two because it was framed as having a higher purpose.

Several years ago, Andrew Kimball issued a call: "Economists, politicians, union leaders, employers, activists, the media—everyone needs to create a new vision of how we earn our livelihoods." New visions require new insights. New insights typically come from sages. A while back, a hospital board asked me to address the question of how ethics might be a more persuasive tool. I brought in two stools, one with three legs and the other with two. It's obvious you can't sit on a two-legged stool, but I used it to reframe how they imagined ethics as part of rhetoric.

Aristotle introduced *rhetoric*, which has to do with persuasion. Corporate America spends billions annually hoping to persuade colleagues to do the right thing. But Aristotle said rhetoric stands on three legs, *ethos, pathos,* and *logos.* Pathos is the ability to appeal to the audience's emotions—to connect with them in a visceral way. Logos has to do with a moral order, a code, our moral DNA. Ethics is the third leg, from the Greek *ethos*, meaning *integrity.* It's seeing emotions and morals as seamless with the way we live. In effect, I suggested a different way to diagnose ethics by connecting it to pathos and logos. I connected ethics to a moral code, ought-is-can-will.

A sage's expertise is diagnosis, which has the idea of seeing *through* a situation to the source of the problem. C-level leaders typically see *to* a situation, reacting to the symptoms that are the *result* of a problem. I'm working with a company where the management system is suffocating. I can pull the lens out and ask whether modern management theory is humane. If management is based on an inaccurate assessment of human nature, every management solution will fail. It's usually a sage who poses these kinds of questions. It's also why wise sages are Socratic—they ask questions and are not afraid to admit that the answers might be difficult to find.

A sage can help C-level leadership decipher E=cc and begin to design a better financial incentive system. Mentors recognize that the problem with incentives isn't that they *don't* work—it's that they work *too* well. After Sarbanes-Oxley, paying CEO's with options has proven to motivate their behavior—they cheat more. Paying teachers according to test scores *does* work—too many teach to the test and cheat students. Incentives do work, but clear-eyed organizations find mentors who understand organizational and human nature well enough to help leaders develop incentive systems that properly influence organizational performance. Otherwise, the company culture is driven by money, and deciphering the moral DNA becomes wink-wink, nod-nod.

Discounting our moral DNA along with the need for a Merlin is the result of a system perfectly designed to marginalize moral considerations. Most management consultants have earned business degrees that are based primarily on the quantitative nature of reality. So have most CEOs and leadership in Corporate America. A Merlin takes into account the reality that numbers can explain much of the arrangement of the world around us, yet he or she defines reality in broader terms. Clear-eyed organizations see the value of this.

Companies with a clear-eyed conscience also recognize the limits of our modern educational system and appreciate that wise sages usually come from outside the business world. Matthew Stewart writes as a sage today. In a former life, he was a principal and founding partner of a consulting firm that eventually grew to 600 employees. But Stewart didn't have an M.B.A. He didn't have extensive business experience. "I have a doctoral degree in philosophy—nineteenth-century German philosophy, to be precise," he writes. Yet this is exactly what made him a wise sage. When he began to read business literature, Stewart saw *through* it—finding it to be disturbingly out of sync with human nature. Silly sayings such as "out-of-the-box thinking," "win-win situation," and "core competencies" simply did not reflect an accurate assessment of human nature. Stewart notes:

> As I plowed through tomes on competitive strategy, business process re-engineering, and the like, not once did I catch myself thinking, Damn! If only I had known this sooner! Instead, I found myself thinking things I never thought I'd think, like, I'd rather be reading Heidegger! It was a disturbing experience.

Stewart's consulting firm upended many business assumptions. For example, they believed modern management theory is fundamentally flawed. Only a Merlin would suggest something this unorthodox. Yet this is exactly what we need across the board—in education, science, politics and public policy; every institution. In the battle over bioethics for example, if sages held a respected place at the roundtable, they'd point out that technology was once a branch of moral philosophy, not of science. A moral code governed technology, arguing that just because something *can* be done does not necessarily mean we *ought* to do it. Without a moral code we're left with *scientism*, which Webster defines as "the methods of the natural sciences" becoming the *only methods that can fruitfully be used in the pursuit of knowledge*. Scientism argues that if something *can* be done it *ought* to be done.

There are sages who see trouble in this. In the April 2008 issue of *Wired* magazine, Bill Joy, cofounder and chief scientist of Sun Microsystems raises questions about unfettered technology and calls for attending to the unintended consequences. The same warning was sounded in the *New Atlantis* article, "The Scientist and the Poet," by Paul A. Cantor, a professor at the University of Virginia. "Science can tell us how to do something, but it cannot tell us whether we should do it. To explore that question, we must step outside the narrow range of science's purely technical questions, and look at the full human context and consequences of what we are doing. To fill in our sense of that context and those consequences, literature can come to the aid of science."

Stepping outside the standard range of questions calls for sages. The President's Council on Bioethics originally played this role, but it was recently reconfigured in favor of a more "practical" approach to bioethical issues. Stay tuned—we could be vulnerable. The problem, as the sagacious Neil Postman put it in his book, *Technopoly: The Surrender of Culture to Technology*, is that technology "does not invite a close examination of its own consequences." A mentor might suggest reading *Faust* by Johann Wolfgang von Goethe. The great poet was also a scientist. "The worthiest professor of physics would be one who could show the inadequacy of his text and diagrams in comparison to nature and the higher demands of the mind," Goethe wrote. Only a sage would suggest that science, or scientism, is inadequate to address the questions raised by emerging technologies. Science needs a roundtable.

Seated at the table, mentors offer diagnosis. But they're not divine. Sages are not perfect. They are perceptive about reality. But a Merlin will still make mistakes. I call sages "80/20" people. Eighty percent of the time they are close to the truth, if not spot on. Twenty percent of the time they're off the mark. That's a pretty good batting average in baseball. Any baseball team, even the Washington Nationals, would see the value of having Merlin's bat in the lineup.

When sages are off the mark, they're clear-eyed in what they ought to do—they're not inflated or inward-bound. When they screw-up, they listen carefully and clear up their mess. They have high EQ. They admit mistakes. Clear-eyed people don't deflect, explain, apologize, hem and haw, blame, justify, or duck the issue. They don't say, "If I've offended anyone, I apologize." Wise sages say, "I blew it." After confession, sages reconcile accounts. That's why sages are often confessors for others—leaders notice that, when a Merlin blows it, he or she makes amends and rectifies the problem.

This kind of candor raises the question of how much value a company's leadership should put on the contribution of a Merlin. When you consider the billions that Corporate America fritters away on consultants, you could make an argument that every company ought to hire a Merlin and pay them at a level close to what the corporate leadership makes. They are that critical to the long-term success of innovative companies.

A Merlin can also enhance the finding of good consultants such as Jim Collins. Collins assigns most of the rise and fall of companies to arrogance. A more full-orbed understanding of human nature reveals that just as many organizations probably collapse due to inward-bound and/or shattered consciences. All three kinds of conscience are in play, creating unhealthy cultures that make long-term innovation unlikely.

Such a nuanced view of human nature and reality rarely makes it to the boardroom. That's because few Merlins get their foot in the door in Corporate America. Most companies tip their hand when they regard Merlin as nothing more than a moralist. Or they look to consultants who are essentially overpriced gurus. How many corporate leaders realize that the buzzwords and catchphrases used by today's most fashionable gurus—"empowerment," "passionate people," "the new organization"—all hail from an assessment of human nature originally springing from Frederick Winslow Taylor and blossoming with his protégés? C-level leaders rarely recognize these consultants as poor imitations of the real thing, wise philosophers and sages, because they lack a second leader at the roundtable—a crap detector.

How would a company discern whether a consultant is a wise sage or simply another in a long line of silly gurus? They'd need a second person at the roundtable. This kind of individual is just as important as a sage—but perhaps even more so. For they are the kind of leader that tells the rest of the roundtable whether this so-called sage is actually full of crap.

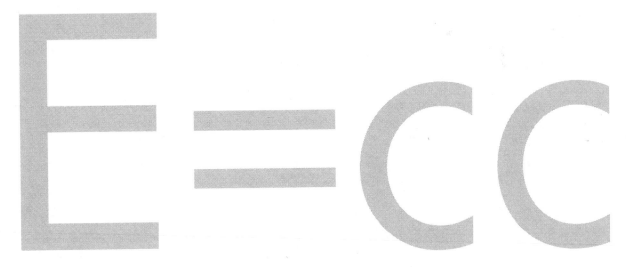

35

CRAP DETECTOR
Human Energy = Is x Clear-eyed

> To be rooted is perhaps the most important and least recognized need of the human soul.
>
> —*Simone Weil*

Most organizations are not rooted in reality.

In the early 1960s, French President Charles de Gaulle flew across the Atlantic to convey a particularly urgent message to the new American President, John F. Kennedy. De Gaulle's concern was Vietnam, where France had lost countless lives and then pulled out in 1954. *You don't understand what you're getting into* was essentially his advice to Kennedy. But Kennedy was cocksure and ignored it. Most people imagine Kennedy as a can-do leader and his cabinet as Camelot. But his roundtable of "the best and the brightest" was arrogant. They lacked crap detectors, or what medieval kingdoms called court jesters. A crap detector is a good thing; the result of multiplying *is times clear-eyed.*

There's an ancient proverb that reads: "Do not be excessively righteous and do not be overly wise. Why should you ruin yourself?" Conscience is a strong concoction that can go straight to the head—even a clear-eyed conscience. Good people can start to read their press clippings. The solution however is not "moderation in all things" but a sense of humor in most things. From time immemorial, the safeguard against smugness has been satire. In the Middle Ages, the court jester played this role. Clear-eyed cultures have court jesters. But this tradition goes further back than the Middle Ages.

In the ancient Near East, poking fun at institutional and individual folly was a virtue. The idea is that success can ruin people by making them excessively (and insufferably) righteous. The same goes for kingdoms. The safeguard was spoof. Satire is spread throughout the Jewish scriptures as a check against myopia and maniacal behavior. Old Testament prophets spoofed idol-worshipers. Elijah ridiculed the prophets of Baal and psalmists decried idols as essentially emperors without clothes. Humor makes hard truths more palatable. Satire isn't assuming an "us versus them" stance against your detractors. It's saving the life of a king or a country by spoofing arrogance or blind spots.

Life-saving send-ups are also a legacy of Western civilization. For example, *In Praise of Folly* was Desiderius Erasmus's satirical stab at the shortcomings of the upper classes and religious institutions of that day. In *A Modest Proposal*, Jonathan Swift's satirical essay from 1729, he suggests that the Irish eat their own children. He was attacking the country's leadership and their indifference to the plight of the desperately poor. In *The Shortest-Way with Dissenters*, Daniel Defoe presented a world in which freedom of religion had become nothing more than the freedom to conform. He was advocating for freedom of conscience. DeFoe was eventually arrested for seditious libel, tried and sentenced to three days in the pillory. Satire is risky business.

The risk is that satire can corrode into sarcasm. Sarcasm is insult and injurious (from the Greek "tearing the flesh"). Satire is insight that pokes fun. A funny bone is helpful in fending off fanaticism or smug self-seriousness. That's why court jesters don't jeer— they aren't angry or cynical. In my opinion, David Letterman seems to be a cynic, who, in the fine phrase of Oscar Wilde, knows the price of everything but the value of nothing. Satire isn't cynical. The British writers Malcolm Muggeridge, who was the editor at *Punch & Judy* from 1953-57, and G. K. Chesterton set the bar for jest. In America, Mark Twain remains the greatest American satirist. His novel *Huckleberry Finn* turned the antebellum South's moral values on its head.

Even the Mafia sees the need for a crap detector. In Mario Puzo's *Godfather*, a consigliore was the chief advisor to Mafia leadership. The word consigliore is often humorously and ironically applied to anyone who serves C-level leadership by helping them see reality. But a chief advisor is generally careful about *who* they mock. A court jester rarely mocked Merlin. He mocked the king. In the same way, a wise court jester mostly points his or her barbs at a CEO or C-level leadership. A crap detector keeps the conscience of pragmatic and visionary leaders clear-eyed. They point out inconvenient truths and potential problems that others are inclined to overlook because considering critiques slows down the success train.

When Ernest Hemingway was asked to identify the essential ingredient required for a great writer, he replied that a person must have a built-in, shockproof crap detector. Marshall McLuhan was a crap detector. He was a media expert who repeatedly challenged conventional management clichés regarding how people and organizations behave and change. For example, in consulting with the likes of IBM, Westinghouse and General Electric, McLuhan noticed that when businesses don't get the preferred results, they ratchet up intensity (he called this "heating up"). Yet intensity reduces peripheral vision, making companies less clear-eyed than before. Passion hardens mental models, making it difficult to change assumptions and outlooks. The Kennedy administration's experience in Vietnam is a tragic example.

McLuhan's solution for organizations was "integral awareness"—the ability to confront what Jim Collins calls the most brutal facts of your current reality, whatever they might be. Integral awareness makes institutions aware of their "rose-coloured glasses" and the inefficacy of many management clichés. Every company needs a few crap detectors, since organizational paradigms "readily become temples into which the light of experience does not enter," Matthew Stewart observes. Even an institution as august as the University of Southern California sees the need for crap detectors.

Since 1991, USC President Steven B. Sample has provided the school with what he calls "contrarian leadership." He institutionalized an appropriate "anti-environment" within the organization itself, a crap detector. A contrarian leader explodes many comfortable views of leadership and suggests unconventional ways to change behavior. Among his counterintuitive lessons: The best leaders don't bother to keep up with the popular media and the trades. Sample provided an "anti-environment" within USC, a contrarian who wasn't afraid to suggest that perhaps the emperor has no clothes. It's one reason why USC has become one of the premier educational institutions in the United States. Under Sample, USC experienced a 25-point jump in the *U.S. News & World Report* annual rankings, going from 51st in 1991 to 26th in 2008. You only get this innovative culture by multiplying *is times clear-eyed* and institutionalizing built-in, shockproof crap detectors.

Has your company institutionalized a crap detector? When personal computers started to hit the market in the 80s, IBM decided to stick with mainframes. Business was good there, with 60 percent margins. Personal computers only enjoyed a 25 percent margin. That turned out to be an unwise decision. But IBM's loss might have been mitigated with a clear-eyed culture. They lacked a crap detector. This indicates that IBM might not enjoy long-term success at being truly innovative.

Past success is one of the best predictors of future failure. I once visited with the CEO of a very successful company. As we toured his headquarters, we came across one of the company posters listing their Core Values, one of which was "Excellence." He was excited until I pointed out that the poster was hung improperly and there was a crack in the wall. "Wow! I never saw that!" Blindness is indicative of a lens that has blurred reality. I was playing the part of a courteous court jester.

It's instructive to remember that Steve Jobs started all over with the iPod while its sales were soaring. He was thinking long-term success. Jobs wasn't drinking the Kool-Aid but rather saw the need to change if Apple was to be truly innovative over the long haul. He probably has a court jester asking hard questions.

The problem in today's companies is that they rarely institutionalize crap detectors. Rather, the contrarian is often written off as not being a "team player." Or a court jester risks being fired when ridiculing ridiculous ideas. No organization has perfumed poop. Court jesters ridiculed the king simply to keep him in touch with reality. But they did not risk the king's wrath or their own life when they multiplied *is times clear-eyed.*

Over the years I have facilitated many forums for middle management. In organizations lacking court jesters, I see eyes roll when the grunts—those working below the managers—hear that company leadership is committed to building a clear-eyed culture. I hear them mutter "*Bullshit.*" This is indicative of an organization with an insulated C-level culture lacking a court jester. They won't be innovative over the long haul.

You can hire a court jester as a consultant. Or, on rare occasion, you might find one or two in the organization. They're rare because most organizations jettison jesters before they can climb the corporate ladder. They're vital because crap detectors can distinguish between sages and silly gurus. Crap detectors keep C-level leaders from drinking their own Kool-Aid and drifting off to La-La Land. Self-deception always tastes good at first.

The bottom line is that a combination of Merlin and court jesters made King Arthur a good king and the kingdom a good kingdom. In fact, Merlin and court jesters are what made the noble knights noble. That's the third kind of clear-eyed individual—a principled pragmatist, or what was known as a noble knight.

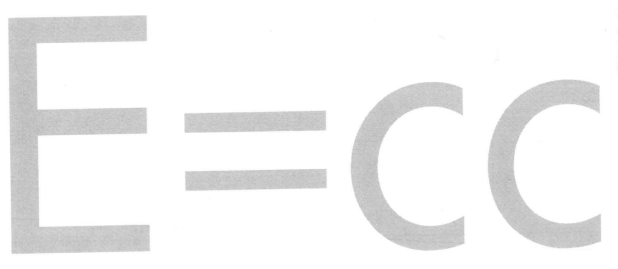

36

PRINCIPLED PRAGMATIST
Human Energy = Can x Clear-eyed

> Virtue is the attempt to pierce the veil of selfish consciousness and join the world as it really is.
>
> —*Iris Murdoch*

If you are a woman, do you like being seen as an easy mark?

If you're looking to buy a car, that's reality. On average, salespeople know they can make more money selling the same make and model to a woman than a man. Women are generally less knowledgeable than men when it comes to knowing a car's true value— and salespeople know it. But even though a salesperson *can* make more, is this the way autos *ought* to be sold? At least one dealership says "No."

At Flow Motors, headquartered in Winston-Salem, North Carolina, they see selling cars as more of a human transaction than a financial one. They view the auto industry as a moral enterprise more than a monetary endeavor (by the way, they have been very profitable over the years). Don Flow is the CEO of Flow Motors and has a vision for selling and servicing cars in a dignified way. This kind of a car culture requires multiplying *can times clear-eyed.* That's innovative; but it's not easy.

Car dealers and Congress rank among the lowest institutions when it comes to being trustworthy. Salespeople tend to be can-do pragmatists who are utterly pragmatic. Flow Motors is out to produce principled pragmatists. For example, every salesperson is trained to treat a woman who walks into the showroom as if that individual was their mother, spouse, or significant other. They don't take advantage of buyers who might be clueless about a catalytic converter. But treating customers with dignity starts with a culture that treats salespeople and mechanics with dignity. Flow notes:

> We have employee gyms and we have a college scholarship foundation program for all of our employees' children. They all get college scholarships. We have a housing assistance program for all entry-level employees. If they save money, we match their down payment to buy a house. We try to pay our people a good wage. But in the end, it can't be just about these things—it must extend to treating each employee as a valued, respected person.

In King Arthur's Court, the can-do, get-it-done go-getters were the Knights of the Roundtable. But because they sat at the roundtable, they were *principled* pragmatists. They were *noble* knights. Companies only get noble knights, or noble salespeople, by multiplying *can-do times clear-eyed.* It's an integral part of innovation.

Principled pragmatists are clear-eyed. They see the entire ought-is-can-will code, even though they are can-do people. They recognize that just because you *can* do something, it doesn't mean you *ought* to do it. This was the challenge facing a group of principled pragmatists that you were introduced to in chapter 16—the Clapham group.

In the 1700s, the English Slave Trade sustained the English economy. "Practical" people accepted it as a necessary evil, a fact of life. The Clapham sect disagreed. Their unique contribution to abolition was tying market systems to moral issues, making a far more persuasive argument than did previous abolitionists. William Wilberforce and his colleagues understood how institutions—shaped by influential individuals—create cultures that create systems that shape economies. Here is how they did it.

As principled pragmatists, they recognized that English Slave Trade was a fairly simple economic triangle—classic mercantilism. Britain's economy was fueled by sugar, which the British consumed in vast quantities. It was the oil of the eighteenth century. "Besides sweetening the naturally bitter tea, coffee, and chocolate, sugar was used in pastries, puddings, biscuits, and candy, and in making many kinds of liquor. It was a preservative in candied fruit, jam, and marmalade, and a 1760 cookbook had recipes for sugar sculptures. One enthusiastic physician, Dr. Frederick Slare, urged the use of sugar for cleaning teeth," Adam Hochschild writes in *Bury The Chains: Prophets and Rebels in the*

Josiah Wedgwood created dinner plates inscribed with "conversation starters."

Fight to Free an Empire's Slaves. It was a culinary symbol of wealth and refinement.

Growing, harvesting, and refining sugar required hot, humid climates, such as were found in the Caribbean. The British West Indies, however, lacked adequate manpower. African slaves were the necessary solution to the supply chain. During the course of the English slave trade, more than two million slaves were imported from Africa to the Caribbean. Only a quarter survived. The Caribbean was a slaughterhouse.

For years, abolitionists harangued members of the British Parliament concerning the evils of the slave trade. Yet abolitionists' efforts were consistently thwarted because they lacked a pragmatic alternative. After Parliament's 1791 rejection of an abolition bill, a group of activist women published a series of pamphlets urging citizens to stop using sugar. They incorporated markets with morality. One of the booklets sold an estimated 70,000 copies in four months. Men were startled by its success. At least 400,000 homes eventually boycotted sugar. The English poet Robert Southey spoke of British tea as "a blood-sweetened beverage." In several parts of England, grocers reported sales of sugar dropping by a third to a half.

These principled pragmatists overlapped their efforts with wise sages such as William Wilberforce and crap detectors such as the excitable activist Thomas Clarkson. Their combined efforts awakened the conscience of even a clergyman, John Newton. The famous writer of hundreds of hymns had been conspicuously quiet about slavery for

nearly 34 years after retiring from the slave trade. Because of the Clapham roundtable, Newton finally spoke out, publishing a forceful pamphlet, *Thoughts Upon the African Slave Trade* that begins by apologizing for a "confession, which…comes too late…It will always be a subject of humiliating reflection to me, that I was once an active instrument in a business at which my heart now shudders." Even Newton became a noble knight. In 1833, the English slave trade was finally abolished.

Clear-eyed pragmatists see the ought-is-can-will code and think in terms of systems, not simply morality. Moralists tend to approach social problems solely in terms of individual activities. Christian Smith, a sociologist at the University of Notre Dame, found that religious people often overlook this reality. They are drawn to helping individuals more than changing institutions. Worthy as these projects may be, Smith warns that none of them attempt to change the systems or the culture that produces the problem. Religious people tend to dispense Band-Aids rather than build institutions that can change the system. Principled pragmatists see systems. That's why they're innovative over the long haul.

Every system is perfectly designed to achieve the results it is getting. This has implications for sequencing the code and innovating, the most notable of which is that systems have their own logic. They create inevitable realities. For example, one may lament the success of films such as *Super Bad* or *The Hangover,* and yet Hollywood is perfectly designed for just such films. The business model dictates the kinds of films that are going to be given theatrical release. This is the promise of sequencing. It can expand our horizons to see reality in new ways by linking Hollywood pragmatic producers with Merlins and court jesters in a roundtable. We need noble knights producing better films.

Roundtables can prick the conscience of kings and filmmakers. The Clapham roundtable engaged such luminaries as Josiah Wedgwood, who fashioned a dinner plate with the inscription: "Am I Not a Man and a Brother?" They called these pieces "conversation starters," designed to prick the conscience of London's leaders. It worked. They changed the culture by first being court jesters, pointing out the moral hypocrisy of England, and then acting as noble knights by creating new systems. The philosopher Sir James Mackintosh would later write of Wilberforce's legacy: "I never saw anyone who touched

life at so many points. No Englishman has ever done more to evoke the conscience of the British people and to elevate and ennoble British life."

The U.S. auto industry could stand to be elevated and ennobled. This is what Flow Motors aims to do. Their company culture is based on an accurate assessment of human nature—what is critical to the long-term success of truly innovative companies. Their people are principled pragmatists; the product of a culture multiplying *can times clear-eyed.* Does your company have noble knights? Do you have a real roundtable?

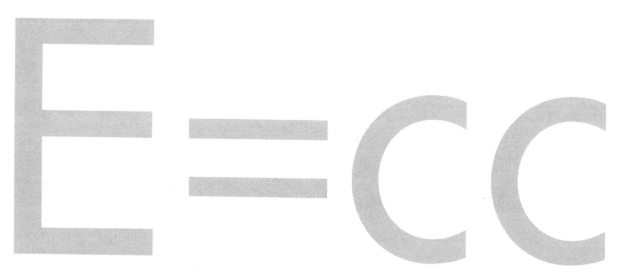

37

VISIONARY
Human Energy = Will x Clear-eyed

> The most important thing anyone can do is to name something.
>
> —*Albert Einstein*

Can you change a self-serious magazine?

In the late 1980s, editors Alan Webber and Bill Taylor tried to change the *Harvard Business Review*. When their boss, Rosabeth Moss Kanter, took a short leave, Webber and Taylor published playful articles such as "Judo Economics," a piece titled "You Just Got Fired," and dozens of other stories that stretched beyond the typical fare swerved in this self-serious magazine. When Kanter returned, Webber and Taylor were told to return to form.

The problem is, they no longer liked the form. They could envision an innovative kind of magazine. When you multiply *will times clear-eyed*, you get visionary leaders. These leaders play the role of kings in companies. But history reveals a few good kings and a bunch of bad ones. King Arthur was a good king, a clear-eyed visionary. But he wouldn't be good without the roundtable. That might have been the problem at *HBR*. Maybe they lacked a roundtable—I wouldn't know for sure. All I know is Webber and Taylor left.

They went out and created a new publication called *Fast Company*, a metaphor for the rapid and continuous change sweeping the business world. A prototype was completed in 1993, and the magazine was launched in November 1995 with a unique take on business. The cover declared *FC* to be the conveyer of "The New Rules of Business." Inside were such category-bending stories as "How to Make a Decision Like a Tribe," "Don't Worry, Be Unhappy," and "Next Time, What Say We Boil a Consultant."

Fast Company has done reasonably well. At the magazine's tenth anniversary in 2005, Webber reinforced the reality that institutions matter—yet they're hard to change. Most of the time, institutions just keep saying the same things over and over. "If you use the same words to describe the world, you're sending the message that nothing's changed," Webber observes. "Change the language, and you change the way people think."

Visionary leaders talk about doing business in a better way. But changing the language is merely the *product* of doing business better. The *process* is deciphering and designing an organization's DNA to ensure long-term success at innovation. Language is a lagging cultural indicator—it does not change the game by itself. It is indicative of the way individuals and institutions see reality. The process of change requires people and organizations reframing reality (I suggest E=cc) and then developing appropriate language. Language always follows.

King Arthur was a visionary leader. But he was a good king because he had his Roundtable. Surrounded by Merlin, court jesters, and noble knights, the kingdom's inhabitant could trust King Arthur's leadership. The Roundtable kept the king tethered to reality. People paid attention to whatever Arthur pronounced to be good. He defined reality.

Albert Einstein said the most important thing anyone can do is to *name something*, to define reality. Visionary leaders *ought* to be in the best position to name reality in an organization. Naming reality, however, requires having the credibility and authority to be listened to and to be taken seriously. Visionary leaders have the authority, but credibility requires a roundtable. When sages, crap detectors, and activists surround C-level leadership, leaders earn the power of "legitimate naming," as Pierre Bourdieu puts it. We need these kinds of leaders who are in touch with reality and are designing companies that contribute to broader social objectives. Corporate America can't be truly innovative over the long haul without these kinds of institutions.

Two-thirds of today's workers say they want business to expand beyond the traditional emphasis on profits and contribute to broader social objectives, according to a Conference Board poll of 25,000 people in 23 countries. "Economist Milton Friedman wrote that the social responsibility of capitalism is to increase shareholder profit,"

Megatrends author Patricia Aburdene writes. "But we've since faced the worst economic crisis since the Depression and begun to experience the consequences of a system that honored profits at all costs. The result of such a philosophy was trillions of dollars in shareholder value being lost." It's time to change the equation and innovate better institutions. How about creating them through sequencing E=cc?

Winston Churchill said we shape our buildings and then they shape us. Individuals matter but institutions shape us even more. We need to decipher and design the DNA of everyday businesses and organizations. Christopher Lasch believed capitalism is *the most significant culture-shaping institution* in the world today. Every organization operates on financial capital, whether it is for-profit or non-profit. Money is the underground aquifer for every institution. If capitalism is better sequenced— creating conscientious capitalism—we can design better ways to offer incentives, do performance reviews, and earn profits. Using E=cc, companies can rethink worker surveillance, hiring practices, and how to mentor workers. Better design of DNA might reduce the annual losses from theft, absenteeism, surfing the Internet, sloppy work, incorrect data entry, drugs, alcoholism—losses that amount to 20 percent of GDP in the United States. Capitalism is not the *only* culture-shaping institution in the world today, but it's probably the most significant. If we redesign capitalism, we redesign institutions and individuals.

This is what visionary leader Dennis Bakke and his business partner, Roger Sant, did in developing AES, an energy distribution company. Bakke recognized that the American workplace was "a frustrating and joyless place where few people do what they're told and have few ways to participate in decisions or fully use their talents." He and Sant envisioned a company capturing the joy a team feels when playing sports. "The first thing we did was to deliberately change our assumptions about people. We said that the assumptions need to be that people are thinking, creative, responsible individuals. And a whole panoply of things have followed from that."

Sequencing that assumption led to requiring colleagues to spend 80 percent of their time on their primary roles and devote 20 percent to participating on task forces, giving advice, learning new skills, and working on special projects. Assuming people are thinking, creative, and responsible meant treating them as having the ability to contribute to deciphering and designing the company's DNA. That's visionary leadership. That's real innovation. Most companies lack this culture. Most CEOs hire can-do pragmatists who can get the job done. But what is the job? *What business are you in?* What is your organization's *ultimate purpose*? The answer suggests whether a company takes its moral DNA seriously or treats it as something nice but not necessary.

So, here we are—almost at the end of the line. What have we sequenced?

Innovation is renewing or changing. Organizations are like marriages; they are either being refreshed or are going stale. They are not static. The reality is that companies never "arrive" at the perfect culture. Culture is dynamic. That's why *long-term* success at being truly innovative is so elusive.

It's true that innovative companies like 3M and Apple do not have to have an accurate assessment of human nature to innovate. Any company can be innovative. But it is almost impossible for companies to enjoy *long-term* success at innovation without an accurate assessment of human nature. That's because people live primarily as enculturated beings; largely unaware of what influences daily decisions and choices. Culture shapes us more than we recognize. But we shape our culture, largely by our conscience.

That's why conscience is critical to the long-term success of truly innovative companies. Conscience is the clearest way to gain an accurate assessment of human nature. When multiplied by the code, you get a better definition of reality.

Meyer's Law says it is a simple task to make things complex, but a complex task to make things simple. E=cc is simple. But don't let the simplicity fool you. Simplicity is the result of rightly subtracting. "Addition is the exercise of fools. Subtraction is the exercise of genius," says Tom Peters. Your colleagues need a way to decipher your company's culture in a compelling fashion. They need a new way to *name reality*. E=cc is simplicity without being simplistic. It is reducing reality to its raw material.

You can't change the equation unless your company has a clear-eyed conscience. Every other kind of conscience—inflated, inward-bound, shattered—invariably results in companies that build levees to bracket institutional and individual behavior. But you can't build a clear-eyed company for the long haul unless *your leadership* is characterized by clear-eyed conscience.

So… now what?

Thomas Kuhn introduced the idea of a paradigm shift. He said it first requires repenting of your past paradigm. The first step in deciphering your company's DNA is recognizing the limits of levees and no longer building them as a buttress to produce better behavior. They don't work. The second step is taking seriously the conundrum of conscience. What's that? If conscience is a lens, and my lens is all I have to see reality, how can I be confident that I'm seeing reality clearly? It's a conundrum, but there is an answer. We'll take it up in Part Four. Once you consider the conundrum of conscience, you can answer two critical questions: Am I clear-eyed? Is my company clear-eyed?

If you complete the sequence of E=cc, you should have deciphered your company's DNA and largely determined if your company can enjoy long-term success at being truly innovative.

FOUR

NOW WHAT?

Taking E=cc Seriously

When we look out through the next hundred years ... the only thing that can defeat us is our own disunity. What drive us together in the first place are our own interests and, even more deeply, our "common values."

Statesmen are fond of stressing these "common values" at the end of their speeches. But over the years our ability to state these values has grown weaker and weaker.

—Michael Novak

38

THE LIMITS OF LEVEES

> That's when it dawned on me: we need a new language. The critical distinction is not between business and social, but between great and good.
>
> —*Jim Collins*

Individuals and institutions are not waterways.

As devastating as Hurricane Katrina was, a greater disaster might have occurred had the storm made landfall just 150 miles to the west, where a series of flood-control structures on the Mississippi River are located.

Begun in the 1950s and built where the river makes a sharp ninety-degree left turn, these dams and channels are designed to fight against the natural inclination of the waterway—which is to follow the path of least resistance and find the shortest route to the sea. In this case, the river wants to continue straight ahead, fanning out into the Atchafalaya Basin. That's the nature of the beast . . . and the problem.

Today, those control structures allow 30 percent of the Mississippi River to go south through the Atchafalaya Basin. But we're fighting against Mother Nature. In 1973, a flood forced the U.S. Army Corps of Engineers to open up the Atchafalaya structures to alleviate floodwaters so that New Orleans wouldn't go underwater. The flood undermined the foundation of the Atchafalaya Dam.

At an additional cost of almost $300 million, the corps proceeded with the construction of an additional structure. But since this cuts off most of the river's sediment, the Atchafalaya is scouring deeper into its riverbed, providing an even *steeper* route for the Mississippi. Again, it's the nature of the beast. But it's also a good picture of what's mostly missing from our modern "ethics training" so common in business today.

As we read about the endless litany of ethical breeches and CEO trials, we *do* need external barriers that curb our tendencies. But most remedies like "ethics training" and the Sarbanes-Oxley Act don't seem to get at the nature of the problem—which is that institutions and individuals are not beasts. They have a conscience. Men and women are not waterways with behaviors that can be curbed by levees. The compliance model treats people this way. It's based on an inaccurate assessment of human nature. No matter how many control structures are built, you can't bracket human behavior.

The solution is not signing off or giving up. Virtue is ultimately obedience to the unenforceable. The *code times conscience* deciphers reality and how we can design obedience to the unenforceable. This is why there is hope in a new equation, E=cc. It tells us that the recent economic collapse is not a failure of capitalism. It's a failure of conscience. In fact, capitalism requires clear-eyed conscience. We need conscientious capitalism.

Capitalism and free markets represent a "system oriented to the human mind: *caput* (from the Latin 'head'), wit, invention, discovery, and enterprise," Michael Novak writes. Capitalism "brings institutional support to the inalienable right to personal economic

initiative." Institutions, in other words, are supposed to promote economic initiative—but not initiatives to merely make as much money as they can. Capitalism should develop companies that encourage individuals to make money the right way—earn what they ought to earn. *Ought* is a moral term. You can't promote healthy capitalism and market economies without a moral system. This is why sequencing E=cc is necessary. Building higher levees is not the solution if we want to prevent future misconduct and promote innovation. Corporate America instead needs business leaders of good conscience who use their wits to promote America's "great experiment" of discovery, enterprise, and self-government, as Novak concludes:

> If Tocqueville was correct, that democracies are ever in danger of slipping downward from high ideals in moral and cultural life, it is imperative that the sound ideals animating the business calling—ideals of community, creativity, practical realism, self-discovery, and many others—be more fully articulated. To ignore or cover over the moral dimension of business is to suck wind out of the democratic sail, and to watch the experiment in self-government go slack.

In the sequencing matrix, 75 percent of companies take the moral dimension of business too lightly. Cultures produce the calculus that a company uses to measure success. But "not everything that counts can be counted, and not everything that can be counted counts," Einstein reminds us. Just because a company's culture—doing the right thing, doing no evil, caring about individuals—doesn't lend itself to being easily measured, does not mean it is the "soft stuff" that doesn't matter. This however might be the reason that culture-shaping activities are often relegated to the sidelines under the category of rain dances. We need a better equation that fosters a system of capitalism *doing the right thing* and no longer treating culture as window dressing. Otherwise, the next time economic pressure increases—as it inevitably will—the levee will once again give way.

Once leaders recognize the limits of levees, the paradigm shift is underway. Now they can begin to decipher the DNA of their organization. There is however a core characteristic of conscience that produces a conundrum. Recognizing it is the way you can keep from kidding yourself.

39

THE CONUNDRUM OF CONSCIENCE

> The paradoxical—and tragic—situation of man is that his conscience is weakest when he needs it most.
>
> —*Erich Fromm*

Woody Allen intuitively recognized what Fyodor Dostoevsky didn't.

Allen's *Crimes and Misdemeanors* adds a dimension to an understanding of conscience that Fyodor Dostoevsky's *Crime and Punishment* did not address. In Allen's film, Judah Rosenthal hires a hit man to dispose of a blackmailing mistress. For a while, Judah's conscience troubles him, just as Raskolnikov's did. But not for long. At the end of the film, Judah unburdens his soul and happily gets on with his life.

In other words, Judah Rosenthal *gets away with murder.*

How can he live with himself?

Human conscience is more than a lens; it's also an arbiter. It acts like a judge, alternatively *accusing* and/or *defending* our "take" on reality. The ought-is-can-will code is reality. Any individual can see it. In a perfect world, the role of conscience is to tap you on the shoulder and point out whether your walk matches your talk. For example, I might say I ought not gossip. But if I gossip, conscience is supposed to step in as an arbiter and tell me I'm full of it.

But this reality creates a conundrum. You can see it by remembering the code. Human conscience *ought* to clarify the moral qualities of our actions. If the lens *is* clear-eyed, conscience *can* act as a safeguard and *will* alternatively accuse an individual of where he or she screws up and defend whatever they get right. Ought-is-can-will. In a perfect world, a clear-eyed person is hearing four voices and therefore can be confident that they're 80/20—they get some things right and some things wrong. Their conscience keeps them in touch with reality, rightly accusing and/or defending them when

appropriate. Unfortunately, in real time, life gets a bit more complex and real messy.

In the real world, reality bites. The lens of conscience bends and warps in the warp and woof of real life. The more warped the conscience, the harder it is for individuals and companies to make a proper distinction between right and wrong. But this doesn't slow down the operation of conscience. It keeps humming along. Human conscience is always operational. But now it starts to make some bad judgments. A corrupted conscience will defend my wrongdoing while accusing others of being the problem, even when they are right. Conscience only properly accuses/defends when it is clear-eyed. It is clear-eyed when an individual or a company has a roundtable. Otherwise, their ability to decipher and determine their conscience and moral actions is seriously impaired. In this situation, conscience will misdirect men and women, making them feel *they're* right, even when they're wrong. It will assign to others what is *our* problem—making us feel that *they're* in the wrong. This is a real conundrum. But it's not insurmountable.

The conundrum is not insurmountable if we face the reality of American individualism. Americans like to figure things out on their own. But if conscience is the only lens through which you see reality, *you* are the easiest person to dupe if you try to decipher *your conscience* without receiving adequate outside signals. This same reality holds true for organizations. Your organizational leadership is the easiest to dupe if it tries to decipher its own conscience without receiving enough outside signals. The conundrum of conscience is that *individuals and institutions can't decipher their own conscience on their own.* The solution however is not deeper soul-searching but developing a roundtable.

This challenge is not insurmountable if we also recognize how most companies are launched and evolve. Entrepreneurs typically start with a great idea or product and hire go-get-em, can-do people. Sequencing tells us that these companies operate under half of the code, "can" and "will." They have visionary leaders and pragmatic people. But they don't have a roundtable. There are no sages and crap detectors. Therefore, how would they know if they are clear-eyed? They can't know. Therefore, they won't innovate over the long haul.

There is a remote possibility that someone somewhere in the company will demand that a roundtable be formed. It's better if this call comes from leadership concerned that the current circle is too small. But this doesn't happen very often since C-level leadership can become quite comfortable with a small circle of decision-makers. In the end, these kinds of companies marginalize a Merlin and castigate a court jester. They don't have a roundtable but a closed loop of closed minds. They forget that a physician who treats himself has a fool for a patient.

This is why companies that are unclear about their conscience need to expand their leadership circle; not turn inward. They need to bring whoever is missing into the inner circle—starting with a crap detector. Why start with a court jester?

Jesters are best suited to discern whether so-called business sages and consultants operate with an accurate or *in*accurate assessment of human nature. A crap detector can easily inform the king and knights whether a particular consultant is full of crap. Court jesters can poke fun at silly gurus that C-level leaders often fawn over and fall for.

Bringing in a court jester however takes guts on the part of corporate leadership. The gutsy move however is not just listening to a wise sage or a court jester—it is institutionalizing their contribution. Most crap detectors and wise sages operate on the fringe; they are generally outside the corporate circle. Institutionalizing them means not just getting their foot in the door; it means giving a court jester and wise sage a place at the table—the roundtable. It means paying for their time and talents.

When institutionalizing a wise sage and court jester concerns or frightens the current roundtable of leadership, you're looking at an unhealthy organization. When they fudge and only hire consultants who offer sustaining technologies, you're looking at a company that will not be innovative over the long haul. By definition, few consultants are concerned for the long haul. Only a company that has institutionalized a Merlin, court jester, noble knights, and a king has a clear-eyed conscience and can define reality. They don't fear crap detectors even though they can sound coarse. Inflated organizations find it intolerable to consider that they might be less than clear-eyed or that their gurus might actually be spouting nothing more than silly sayings. Inward-bound organizations can suffer the same pain, finding it too painful to consider that they might be less than clear-eyed or that their so-called mentors are really nothing more than moralists. In both cases, it's highly unlikely these companies will remain truly innovative over the long haul. Everyone needs a roundtable. Otherwise we're in La La Land. I've seen leaders not only lose their integrity, but their organizations lose their ability to innovate over the lack of a roundtable.

I have seen leaders do the wrong thing—lying, character assassination, philandering, pilfering, plagiarism, you name it—and then arrogantly blow off correction or curl up in a fetal position and play the role of victim of unfortunate circumstances when questioned. It is the conundrum of conscience, defending misdeeds, accusing others of being the "real" problem, and being clueless about reality. It's a conundrum because people don't wake up in the morning and say, "Honey, I'm going to be an ass today!" They don't drive to work and think: "How can I destroy this company and the retirement funds of thousands of people?" "How can I lie, cheat, and steal?" But people do these things. They are the unwitting product of an inflated or inward-bound or shattered culture. Their "broken" conscience tells them they are not the problem. Our naïveté regarding the collective impact and force of culture on our sense of right and wrong is the culprit here. This cultural naïveté is reinforced in Corporate America where unbridled visionaries and unprincipled pragmatists hold the reins and ignore conscience.

Seen in this light, human conscience can throw a monkey wrench in the machinery. Conscience is the peculiarly human faculty that enables individuals and institutions to do good or condone evil. Einstein's theory of relativity contributed to the development of nuclear energy that has provided positive dividends. But it also contributed to the development of nuclear explosives that have proven to be unthinkably destructive. The theory of reality, $E=cc$, holds the same promise and potential destruction. We can be brilliant and bad. Companies can be terrible or trustworthy.

In Corporate America, there are millions of transactions occurring daily that are based on mutual trust. Employees go to work today trusting that their employer will pay them accurately and on time later. Few people would ship goods on credit if they didn't trust that they would get paid. As Francis Fukuyama writes in his book *Trust: The Social Virtues and the Creation of Prosperity*, "one of the most important lessons we can learn from an examination of economic life is that a nation's well-being, as well as its ability to compete, is conditioned by a single, pervasive cultural characteristic: the level of trust inherent in the society."

Trust is faith and good faith is not blind. Good faith can only be reliably placed in individuals and institutions of good conscience. The bottom line in deciphering an organization's DNA is deceptively simple: only individuals and institutions of good conscience can promote human flourishing and healthy innovation over the long haul. Businesses have caught on to the erosion of trust and highlighted its importance—and justifiably so. But few, if any, have elevated human conscience to its critical role in innovation.

Think about the last decade. In 2002, we were talking about WorldCom, Enron, Global Crossing, Xerox, Sunbeam, Waste Management, Adelphia, ImClone Systems, and Qwest. These companies dominated the media for that year because of their accounting irregularities, restated earnings, lost value of millions of shareholders' dollars, and for some, bankruptcy. That seems like a long time ago, doesn't it?

What is telling is that many of these companies had one other factor in common: their auditor was Arthur Andersen, the accounting firm that went belly-up in the wake of Enron's collapse. It took 75 years for Arthur Andersen to make a name and 75 days to lose it. The odds are great that Arthur Andersen had a corporate conscience justifying its actions. Conscience presents us with a real conundrum.

Conscience was the conundrum that eventually caused my friend Bill to drop his interest in the code. Wracked by guilt over his offshore shenanigans and sexual flings, Bill began to lie to himself. He saw the code and agreed with it, but when I began to decipher it, he decided a roundtable was too intrusive.

Conscience is the key characteristic that changes the game. The code is reality, ought-is-can-will. Reality is reality. Can't get over it, can't get around it. If my friend Curtis, the plant superintendent from an earlier chapter, is ever going to institutionalize an innovative company culture where crap is no longer the norm, the company is going to have to form a roundtable. How do you do that?

It begins by answering two questions: Am I clear-eyed? Is my company clear-eyed?

40

AM I CLEAR-EYED?

Generalities are the refuge of weak minds.

—*Socrates*

I can decipher conscience by taking names.

Since conscience is an individual's only lens to see reality, and it accuses or defends, *you* are the easiest person to dupe if you try to decipher *your own conscience on your own.* So how can you tell if you are clear-eyed? The answer is a roundtable.

When a friend tells me that he or she lives with a clear-eyed conscience, I ask if they have a roundtable. If they say yes, I ask for names, phone numbers, and email addresses of their four friends—sages, crap detectors, pragmatists, and visionaries. If they are indignant at my asking this question, I'm probably looking at an inflated conscience. If the person acts like they've been invaded, I'm probably looking at an inward-bound conscience. If they flip the bird at me, I'm probably looking at a shattered conscience.

Socrates said generalities are the refuge of weak minds. I find that by asking for King Arthur's Roundtable that includes a Merlin, court jesters, noble knights and a king; I'm getting down to brass tacks. Too often, people form accountability groups that are little more than group hugs or composed of yes-men (or yes-women). Roundtables have four particular kinds of people. Properly sequencing E=cc keeps us from simply pureeing people into an undifferentiated pool of pals who never cut it straight with you. By collecting names, phone numbers, and email addresses, I can contact a friend's roundtable and learn whether or not these individuals see themselves playing the role of a Merlin, court jester, noble knight, or king. If they scratch their head and are clueless, I know my friend lacks a roundtable.

I have a roundtable. One of my court jesters is a CEO who cuts it straight with me when

I need it (which is often). Many years ago, one of his company's colleagues flew in from China for a short visit. After dinner, I took this colleague aside and basically told him how the world rotates. After he retired for the night, my friend asked me: "Man, what's wrong with you?" It was a slap in my face, and I needed it.

I also have a Merlin or two. "Unlike other animals, people do have a drive to seek coherence and meaning," David Brooks writes. "We have a need to tell ourselves stories that explain it all." Merlins tell me stories through which I can decipher my conscience. Do you have a Merlin? Years ago, I was fixated on growing my organization as fast as possible. My wise sage casually mentioned: "Tumors grow too." In fact, tumors are some of the fastest growing organisms in your body. I needed my Merlin to mention that perhaps fast growth wasn't the main end.

These stories take on a positive patina over time. But they were painful back then. Friends *are* painful. They don't let friends live in La-La Land. As one writer put it, "Faithful are the wounds of a friend." In our therapeutic age, we need a more positive view of pain. The pioneering work with leprosy of Seattle surgeon Paul Brand changed much of my thinking about pain.

Brand was born in India in 1914 to British missionary parents. Growing up, he saw firsthand the horrible effects of leprosy. But Brand was the first physician to discover that leprosy was actually a disease, the destruction of nerve endings that made sufferers susceptible to injury. The rotting away of tissues was due to the loss of the sensation of pain. Lepers would routinely place their hands on hot stoves or smash fingers with hammers. The loss of pain in the limbs meant the eventual loss of those limbs.

Brand concluded that to live without pain is to live in constant peril. He became grateful for pain, seeing it and gratitude as inextricably linked. We need a new generation of leaders who are grateful for roundtables that occasionally hurt when sages wisely pull the lens out, see patterns, and ask larger questions... and when court jesters cut through the crap. We need to be reminded of King Arthur's Roundtable.

The Englishman Samuel Johnson said people more often need to be reminded than informed. Paul Brand discovered the more people are inoculated against pain, the less they can tolerate it. It's worth remembering that Americans consume well over 95 percent of the pain-killing drugs available in the world. As a result, Americans have the lowest pain tolerance of all countries in the world since attitudes towards pain greatly influence the use of drugs. Pain is a gift, but nobody wants it. Getting a real roundtable will, at times, prove to be painful. But the more you experience pain, the less you fear it and the more you appreciate it.

At the close of *Saving Private Ryan*, there is a scene weighted with gravitas. Having survived the war but knowing many soldiers died to save him, the elderly Ryan collapses before the Normandy grave of one of his fallen comrades. Struggling to get up, he asks his wife: "Tell me I'm a good man. Tell me I've lived a good life." At this poignant moment, he didn't want his spouse blowing smoke up his rear. He wanted reality. The incredible potential in $E=cc$ and the conundrum of conscience means you don't need people offering inane accolades when the weight of reality is weighing on you. Do you feel the weight of reality? Do you feel the incredible potential for good because human beings have a conscience? Do you feel the terrible potential for delusion and evil because human beings have a conscience? When you feel the gravitas of reality, you don't want glad-handed accolades. You want a roundtable.

Reality is reality. The answer to the second question—is my company clear-eyed?—is the same as the answer to the first question. You don't want inane accolades when you're asking whether you have a good organization. You want a roundtable. In King Arthur's day, if one or more was missing, the kingdom was in trouble.

41

IS MY COMPANY CLEAR-EYED?

> The most important power we have is the power to select the lens through which
> we see reality.
>
> —*David Brooks*

You can't choose your DNA. But you can choose the lens through which you see reality.
The bottom line however is that maintaining a clear-eyed conscience is not primarily
about making choices. The reality is that, at the moment of choosing, most of the choices
have already been made. It is impossible to stay clear-eyed if an individual lives and works
for a long time in an organization that is not. The environments in which we spend most
of our lives shape us. Institutions are more powerful than individuals.

One of my friends in the investment business runs a small practice. I asked him whether
his company had a clear-eyed conscience. "I think so." Then I asked him for the names,
phone numbers, and email addresses of his wise sages, crap detectors, principled
pragmatists, and visionaries. "Uh…," he replied.

Conscience is our only lens to see reality. Since it accuses or defends, the conundrum is
that *an organization* can easily be duped if its leadership tries to decipher the company's
conscience on its own. Only by having the same roundtable that an individual *must have*
can an institution decipher if it is clear-eyed. Where are the wise sages, crap detectors,
principled pragmatists, and visionaries? Can you give me their name, rank, and serial
numbers?

Only organizations with clear-eyed cultures are trustworthy. Harris poll data shows
that only 27 percent of Americans trust government. The numbers for Congress are
alarming—as low as nine percent in 2008. Twenty-two percent trust the media, nine
percent trust political parties, and—inside organizations—only 51 percent trust their

C-level leadership. That's because few organizations have a roundtable that makes the firm reliable. Too many companies treat culture like cotton candy. But culture is a social control system that is already operating inside every organization. Culture is like a diet. No one goes *on* a diet. Diet is everything you eat and how much you exercise—the good, bad, and ugly. You *are* on a diet right now. Your company has a culture, right now. Yet few are aware of it. It's why so few companies actually change their culture. Sequencing E=cc will determine whether your company can innovate for success.

Of the dozens of firms that John Kotter has studied over the years, he found that only ten had succeeded in enterprise-wide culture change. This included GE, Xerox, and British Air. But even these success stories can prove short-lived. It takes ten years on average to change the culture of a company. Individuals and organizations understand this dynamic in reframing expectations.

In 2004, Joe Ehrmann was featured on the cover of *Parade* magazine as "The Most Important Coach in America." A former All-American at Syracuse who played for the Baltimore Colts, Joe's purpose then was winning games. Now his purpose in life is making men. On Friday nights before football games, parents typically ask: "Joe, how are we going to do tonight?" *We'll know in thirty years* is his reply. Ehrmann recognizes that making men requires making culture. It takes time. It requires continually tilling the soil. Culture, like agriculture, is long-term, never-ending work.

Culture is probably the most stubborn, difficult characteristics to change inside a firm. Clear-eyed cultures give voice and authority to wise sages, crap detectors, principled pragmatists, and visionaries. Otherwise, institutions begin to act like Lake Wobegon, where everyone is above average. But that can't be. That's not reality.

I was recently visiting with a CEO who has seen the E=cc matrix. "I think I'm a man of clear-eyed conscience and know that my #2 certainly is." Unfortunately, that's not what I was hearing from others in the company. My fear is that visionaries, as in most companies, hire unprincipled pragmatists and these two primarily populate C-level leadership. In a clear-eyed culture, this CEO would also institute wise sages and crap detectors at the roundtable. In fact, in a clear-eyed culture, C-level leadership would be *demanding* that wise sages and crap detectors be given a place at the roundtable. That's not currently happening. Insularity invites inaccurate assessments.

Most companies become comfy with their culture and are not in a very good position to decipher their culture. Deciphering a culture is a lot like asking someone to describe the contact lenses they are wearing. The most comfortable contacts are those we are *unaware* of. At age 47, I started to wear reading glasses. I've never gotten comfortable with them. But if I had worn them from Day One, I'd probably be like most people who do become comfy with their corrective lenses and hardly give them any thought.

If C-level leadership feels threatened when asked for names and email addresses of their roundtable, that's indicative of an inward-bound conscience and culture. When these inward-bound leaders shape an organization's culture, they take the whole firm hostage. If C-level leadership acts insulted when asked for names and email addresses of their roundtable, that's indicative of an inflated conscience and culture. In these companies, C-level leaders create a culture of deference rather than directness. It's not a clear-eyed culture. In both cases, you're looking at a firm full of unprincipled pragmatists and visionaries. They need to complete the roundtable with wise sages and crap detectors.

As with individual assessments, organizations are wise to bring in sages and crap detectors from outside to assess reality. It's too easy for corporate leadership to be self-deluded or insulated. This, by the way, is one of the problems with age-specific organizations, such as "Gen-Ex" institutions. I worked briefly with an organization that targeted only 20- and 30-year-olds. Focus is fine, but over time I watched their leadership become dismissive of what older sages bring to the table. It's easy to sound like a wise sage when no one in the room is older than 35. All you're really doing is pooling ignorance. That organization is becoming cocksure—but I bet they don't see it because they are only receiving input from visionaries and pragmatists.

If organizations are serious about deciphering their DNA, Merlins and court jesters can be brought in. My business partner and I routinely play these roles in organizations. John tends to also be a wise sage as well as a noble knight. He's even a king, developing a couple of companies as a social entrepreneur. I'm better at seeing patterns and problems. We help firms form roundtables.

This might sound self-serving, since consultants are famous for creating needs that

supposedly only they can meet. That's not the case here. There are probably hundreds if not thousands of sages and crap detectors available to Corporate America. I've laced my company with a few. In other words, as I mentioned in the previous chapter, I take my own medicine. In my organization, I strive to have a roundtable board populated by Merlins, court jesters, knights, and kings. The CEOs on my board tend to function as kings, promoting the vision of my organization. Others are can-do, get-it-done principled pragmatists. One or two are crap detectors. A medical doctor and a CEO on my board often play the role of Merlin.

Your company, by itself, cannot determine whether it has a clear-eyed conscience. I can't say it enough: the organization you can most easily dupe is *your* organization. The problem for most firms is not reality *per se*, but individual perceptions of reality. When people don't like the view, they often tint the glasses and their "take" on reality. Only court jesters can correct rose-colored glasses.

The brutal reality is that most organizations lack the Camelot culture to be truly innovative over the long haul. It's not that they don't *want* to. It's that they *cannot* innovate. Cannot. They think they can, believe they can, even imagine that they are. But they can't. They don't operate with an accurate assessment of human nature, which is critical to the long-term success of truly innovative companies. That's reality. They're sticking with the same numbers but rearranging 1+2+3 into 3+2+1 and expecting a different result. All innovation requires creative destruction. Most businesses are incapable of voting for their own obsolescence. *Incapable*. Once a culture is in place, it's very difficult to tear down. No one understood this better than Robert Moses.

Moses started out in 1914 as a passionate reformer of New York's corrupt Tammany Hall. "In those pre-World War I years of optimism, of reform, of idealism, Robert Moses was the optimist of optimists, the reformer of reformers, the idealist of idealists," biographer Robert A. Cato writes. Moses believed that great ideas would form new values and that Tammany Hall would be moved to act on them. Tammany Hall did. They fired Moses in 1918.

Ten years later Moses was back in New York, a different man. "When the curtain rose on the next act of Moses' life, idealism was gone from the stage. In its place was an

2052 205 · Sequencing understanding that ideas—dreams—were useless without power to transform them into reality." Moses became a creator of culture, the "master builder" of New York City. He never held an elected office, but at the height of his power, "between 1946 and 1953, no public improvement of any kind—no school or sewer, library or pier, hospital or catch basin—was built by any city agency unless Moses approved its design and location."

The clearest example of the power of culture was when Moses built his new parkways. He wanted to give New Yorkers a break from Manhattan's sweltering summer. The answer was Long Island's beaches—but not for everyone. Moses was a racist; he considered African-Americans inherently "dirty." So he ensured his parks would be largely inaccessible to them by engineering the Long Island bridges with maximum headroom of 13 feet in the middle, yet only 11 feet at the curb. Most of New York's African-Americans rode buses that were taller than 11 feet but had to drive on the curb lane on parkways. For a bus to make it to a state park, it had to navigate long and arduous back roads. Few people however objected to Moses' bridges because they looked so beautiful. Moses knew that once the bridges were in place, it would cost untold millions to replace them.

It works the same with cultures—they are hard to tear down. Most C-level leadership thinks their cultures look pretty good. But a company can only properly decipher their DNA if their conscience *is* clear-eyed and they're receiving four signals.

Biological DNA determines our biology. Behavioral DNA largely determines corporate behavior. Institutional cultures operate like bridges—they prevent or permit individual actions. Firms with clear-eyed consciences tend to achieve higher results because they're working *with* reality and human nature, not against it. Firms with disordered DNA generally focus on problems rather than questioning whether their "take" on reality is accurate. At the end of the day, they're simply recycling old paradigms. Recycling is great for the environment but bad for enterprises. It also makes innovation unlikely over the long haul.

We need companies that do the hard work of creating cultures of clear-eyed conscience. This means getting the right people on the bus, getting them in the right seats, and getting the wrong people off the bus, as Jim Collins says. Rearranging means making a roundtable. Does your organization have a roundtable? Does it have a clear-eyed conscience? "The most important power we have is the power to help select the lens through which we see reality," notes David Brooks. He's right.

If your company claims to be clear-eyed, where is the roundtable of robust wise sages, crap detectors, principled pragmatists, and visionaries? Knowing their name, rank, and serial numbers is the only way you can determine whether your company can enjoy long-term success at being innovative.

Epilogue

42

OUT OF THE ABYSS

> The tragedy of modern man is not that he knows less and less about the meaning of his own life, but that it bothers him less and less.
>
> —*Vaclav Havel*

Clive disappeared—and then reappeared.

In March 1985, Clive Wearing disappeared into an abyss. Struck by a brain infection in his mid-forties—a herpes encephalitis—Wearing was left with an amnesia that wiped out virtually his entire past. Yet one faculty was left totally intact: he recognized tunes.

Wearing was an eminent English musician and musicologist who also enjoyed reading. In an awful irony, *The Lost Mariner* was Clive's book du jour in January 1985—the story of a patient with severe amnesia. Clive's wife, Deborah, had no idea, as she wrote in her 2005 memoir, *Forever Today*, that they were "staring into a mirror of our own future." The infection devastated Clive's brain. Memories of his children and work seemed lost forever, as well as the ability to retain new memories. Clive would say, "It's like being dead."

Clive could still function—shave, shower, dance, talk, read and write in several languages, make phone calls, and find his way about the house. Yet when asked *why* he did particular things, Clive could not recall. He was in an abyss.

Deborah, however, soon discovered that Clive retained two memories. He recognized her and, when she played music, he reemerged from the abyss. He remembered tunes. When handed the two volumes of Bach's *Forty-eight Preludes and Fugues*, Clive at first said that he had never seen or played any of them before. But when he sat down and began to play Prelude 9 in E Major, he said, "I remember this one." He recognized every tune he had ever learned—Handel, Bach, Beethoven, Berg, Mozart, and Lassus—and the playfulness came back. His musical powers were intact. How?

Larry Squire, a neuroscientist who has studied the mechanisms of memory and amnesia, believes that two very different sorts of memory exist: a conscious memory of *particular* events and an unconscious memory of *patterns*. Musical tunes are more like *pattern* memories—they play in our head even if we don't know the lyrics. Lyrics, on the other hand, are more like *particular* memories. Squire says the memory of *patterns* is unimpaired in amnesia. Amnesiacs can recognize a tune, even if they have forgotten the lyrics. Music goes deeply into emotions and memories in ways that words do not.

Has a realistic assessment of human nature disappeared into an abyss? Does this loss account, in part, for our unprecedented problems?

Think about it. The code is exactly like pattern memory—a tune playing in everyone's head. It might sound like *shoulda coulda, woulda*—but it *is* universal. Human beings all over the world, C. S. Lewis wrote, have this curious idea that they *ought* to behave in a certain way, and can't really get rid of it. That's the first note of the code. The second note, writes Hollywood screenwriter Robert McKee, is "the struggle between expectation and reality in all its nastiness"—the way life really *is*. We hear the third note in the stirring speech given by Dr. Martin Luther King Jr. upon receiving the 1964 Nobel Peace Prize. He refused "to accept the idea that the 'isness' of man's present nature makes him morally incapable of reaching up for the eternal 'oughtness' that forever confronts him." We *can* do better, he said. And Nietzsche had the fourth note playing in his head whenever he experienced joy: "All joy wills eternity—wills deep, deep eternity."

Few organizations see reality this way—through ought-is-can-will. Thus, few are sequencing it. Without deciphering this behavioral DNA, institutions probably won't design a culture that *leverages conscience*. What Corporate America needs is capitalism with a conscience, or what I call "conscientious capitalism." If companies aren't leveraging conscience, they're not operating with the rhythms of reality. That's a more accurate assessment of how human nature works. It's how long-term innovation works.

In reality, it's how everyone and every organization works.

If companies begin to sequence E=cc, it might yield better workplaces, better products, better policies—and better people. If they use it to decipher reality and design better workplaces, then we've changed the equation. We're not doing the same thing over and over and expecting a different result. If E=cc is an accurate assessment of human nature, then we're talking about reality in new ways. *That's* innovative.

Computers operate by the binary code—zeros and ones. Biology operates by DNA—our molecular material. Behavior operates by the *code times conscience*, our moral material. The critical component is *not* the ought-is-can-will code, however. It is *conscience*, both corporate and individual.

Every institution, company, or organization has a conscience. The question is, which conscience is most likely to ensure long-term success at being truly innovative? Only a culture characterized by a clear-eyed conscience. The good news about E=cc is that any institution or individual—regardless of race, creed, gender, or color—can discover it through our shared, human experiences. This means any company can sequence E=cc and determine whether it's capable of long-term innovation. E=cc is a shared source of knowledge about reality. Over 100 years ago, the philosopher William James called for a "radical empiricism" as a warrant for taking all kinds of lived experience seriously, as sources of knowledge. When you read "radical," don't think Abbie Hoffman. *Radical* means "from the root." Ought-is-can-will is radical, it's at the root of all behavior. E=cc takes in every kind of lived experience. Properly sequenced, it can change the game.

It can, in fact, change every game. This is a book about reality, not just about business or companies. Reality is reality. That's why the stories have come from across the spectrum of history and everyday life, not just boardrooms or salesrooms. This definition of reality explains what we feel, think, say, and do everyday. Don't think we're only talking about business. We're talking about *life*.

Because this is a book about defining reality, the reality is that it's not the last word. It's only the beginning. Eighty percent of what you have read is close to reality while 20 percent is not close enough. We need crap detectors to join the human nature project and improve on what's been written here. *Sequencing* aims to be realistic, and recognizes we need principled pragmatists to inculcate this definition of reality into organizations. We need visionary CEOs and C-level leaders willing to redesign their company culture, if they want to ensure being truly innovative over time. *Sequencing,* in other words, only sounds the starter's gun. It's not the finish line. It's a launch pad, not a landing pad.

In 1953, Watson and Crick discovered biological DNA. You've just discovered the behavioral code. You've discovered the theory of reality, E=cc.

Now comes the hard part. Who will join the adventure of sequencing? The easiest way to learn your answer is to take a look at your bookmark. How did you answer the question I posed at the beginning of this book? Are you working to make the big bucks or is it more about fulfilling the larger purpose of your organization? If it's the latter, properly deciphering E=cc will improve the odds that your company will enjoy long-term success at being truly innovative.

Does your company have a Camelot culture?

Everyone recognizes that Camelot is a myth. Yet all great myths reflect the deepest reality. Thus, Camelot is more than a myth. It's the dream of all leaders and companies characterized by clear-eyed conscience. King Arthur's Roundtable awaits us.

ABOUT THE AUTHOR

Michael Metzger is the founder and President of The Clapham Institute (www.claphaminstitute.org), a non-profit entity whose mission is to align people and organizations with an accurate assessment of human nature. Its aim is to facilitate long-term institutional innovation. Prior to launching the Institute, Mike was the Executive Director for the Osprey Point Leadership Center, a conference center on Maryland's Eastern Shore.

Before his involvement with Osprey Point, Mr. Metzger worked as a consultant and advisor for dozens of organizations, speaking throughout the United States and Western Europe. He has also been an adjunct instructor at several graduate schools.

The Clapham Institute conducts C-level roundtables throughout the country for institutional leaders and offers consulting services for organizations seeking to be innovative over the long haul.

The Clapham Institute also facilitates Skunk Works—specialized innovation teams—inside organizations or with small groups—Cultural Creatives—within a city. These roundtables are 12-18 months in duration and push individuals and institutions to create innovative products and services that serve the common good.

Finally, The Clapham Institute publishes books and commentary on current topics related to business, technology, art, media, politics, and community development.

Game Changer Books

Challenging the Given for the Greater Good

Game Changer Books is a digital publishing company designed to use innovative technology to foster dialogue on topics that challenge mass culture and dominant consumer trends. It seeks to use the best of digital publishing and viral marketing to create individualized campaigns for books that foster human flourishing and the common good. It is a niche publisher seeking books that challenge prevailing assumptions about society and call for a return to the objective reality of the good, true, and beautiful. Its audience is cultural creatives and institutional gatekeepers.

Please visit: www.gamechangerbooks.com

5392118R0

Made in the USA
Charleston, SC
08 June 2010